Praise for Darren Pierre and
The Invitation to Love:

"Darren takes the reader on a journey - like skipping rocks across a serene lake at dawn - leaving the reader to apply his own life lessons leading to being open to receiving and giving love."

— Jessica Pettitt, Good Enough Now.com

"Honest and inspiring, this gem of a book can change your perspective, attitude, and feelings about yourself and others. It awakens the heart for receiving and giving love."

— Susan Friedmann, CSP, International Best-Selling Author of *Riches in Niches: How to Make it BIG in a Small Market*

"This book is a treasure! It uses stories and personal examples to illustrate an extraordinary view of life and the relationships that make it worth living. When you practice the perspectives offered in this book, you will find your life greatly enriched."

— Tracy Maxwell, Author *Being Single, with Cancer*

"As a gay, black man from a broken home, Darren Pierre has experienced the feeling of not being enough, battled with self-esteem and relationship issues, and experienced love's pain, but he has also pushed aside resentment, found wholeness in forgiveness, and now shares his lessons about love with others. His courageous spirit, gentle soul, and words of truth will help heal your spirit and inspire you to re-embrace the beauty of life and all its possibilities."

— Tyler R. Tichelaar, Ph.D., and award-winning author
of *Narrow Lives* and *The Best Place*

"Powerful, Authentic, Clear, Accessible, Timely and Needed. Darren's work is for anybody who has ever wondered if they are enough. Darren's work offers a healing journey and creates the opportunity for folks to have a "Me Too" moment. The 'Me Too' moment is the one that let's you know you are not alone. In a world with such suffering in isolation, this is a "must read".

— Dr. Jamie Washington, President
of the Washington Consulting Group

"No other read has motivated me so much to look inward and consider my own insecurities both about love and life. As a person who too often suppresses the pain, complications and worry, The Invitation to Love opened my heart to the opportunity of self-reflection, and in that the unfolding of emotion, like a bud in spring. Darren's gift lies in his ability to speak so close to his own soul, a voice so pronounced as you read from chapter to chapter, you feel that he is seated beside you. This book will inspire you."

— Michael Anthony Villasenor,
Creative Director at *The New York Times*

"Every now and then an event happens that makes you realize the true meaning of life. This book can be 'that event' which will completely change your entire perspective. This soon-to-be classic will remind you that love, in its purest sense, is truly a privilege and should always be honored, cherished and kept sacred. Get ready for your future to be forever altered as your relationships will never again be the same!"

— Patrick Snow, Publishing Coach and International Best
Selling Author of *Creating Your Own Destiny*

The Invitation to Love

Recognizing the Gift Despite Fear, Pain, and Resistance

Darren Pierre

AVIVA
PUBLISHING
New York

The Invitation to Love
Recognizing the Gift Despite Pain, Fear, and Resistance

Published by
Aviva Publishing
Lake Placid,NY
(518) 523-1320
www.AvivaPubs.com

Darren Pierre
PO Box 607871
Chicago IL 60660
Darren@theinvitationtolove.com
www.TheInvitationtoLove.com

ISBN: 9781940984865
Library of Congress: 2015901834

Cover Designer: www.AngelDogProductions.com
Interior Book Layout: www.AngelDogProductions.com

Printed in the United States Of America.
First Edition
2 4 6 8 10 12

This book is dedicated to anyone
who has had the faith to dare, the humility to pray,
and the insight to be still in the meantime.

Acknowledgment

With this work,
I acknowledge all who have felt love,
experienced pain, and
then found hope and promise in both.

Content

Section Three: A Healthy Disregard for the Impossible

Preface

This book is a course on love. The students are all of God's children who breathe air, have hearts that sing, and have spirits yearning to be seen. The journey is daunting, full of tears, and led by faith—a gut-wrenching voyage that, if undertaken, transforms the human experience and elevates the soul. The aim of these pages is simple: to guide the reader to an understanding of one person's journey to be liberated from pain, and to discover, and, more importantly, accept the invitation to be and to love.

The tenor of much of what is said within this piece may feel as though it comes from a Judeo-Christian context; that is certainly not intentional. I would not be honest with you or myself if I did not acknowledge that Christianity influences this work and can serve as an effective road map to truth. I will not, however, stand on the stage of arrogance and say that one specific faith tradition is the only way. On the contrary, hundreds of thousands of religious and non-religious figures alike have illustrated and mastered living lives powerfully and in the pursuit of all things true. This work is meant for anyone: Christian, Daoist, Muslim, Hindu, Sikh, Atheist, Buddhist, or holders of any other belief for that matter.

I wrote this book from the perspective of a black, gay man, and while the path I have walked, carrying each of those identities, has influenced this piece, those identities are not intended to limit the scope of the audience who can relate to this book. Whether you are male, female, transgender, black, white, Latino(a), Asian, gay, straight, bisexual, pansexual, disabled, able-bodied, rich, poor, or any other socially constructed identity, this book is for you. The only request I make of the reader is to value truth and to have the courage to move in that space.

This book is formulated as a series of stories. Many of the stories are written from a broad perspective, and at points may seem vague. Each piece is written intentionally so that the story provides enough content for you to make meaning in your own life, but is general enough for vast applicability. The stories are divided into three main sections, the first of which is "Section One: Live in Your Truth." Its aim is to illustrate the power of listening to the greatest, most intelligent voice we will ever know: the voice within. "Section Two: Perseverance" encourages us to stay the course in our journey to love. Marianne Williamson said it best in her book, Enchanted Love, when she shared, "Love will push every button, try every faith, challenge every strength, trigger every weakness, mock every value and then leave you there to die...." The journey is not easy—an honest assessment of the difficulty in identifying and sustaining love's expression is important. "Section Three: A Healthy Disregard for the Impossible[1]" introduces the promise that comes from harnessing faith.

As you read this book, at times these three main points (Live in Your Truth, Perseverance, and A Healthy Disregard for the Impossible) may seem repetitive—that repetition is intentional. The objective is to reiterate these three tenets in myriad ways to drive home each point with the goal to reach a diverse audience. The book is layered, meaning each section builds on the previous, and while the book is formulated as a series of short essays independent of one another, you are asked to read the book in order,

---

[1] I'd like to give the organization LeaderShape®, Inc. credit for coining this phrase I have adopted.

in its entirety, to get a full understanding of the message being conveyed.

The stories and experiences I will share are at times heart-warming, while at other points heartbreaking; however, I believe that diversity is what gives life its beauty. I pray the reader is able to see the power of love, the tenacity it takes to persist, and the ability to foster faith through it all. I hope the words that populate these pages nurture your own voyage to love's manifestation. I give you my deepest gratitude for joining me on this journey.

Introduction

My own journey in learning what it means to love has not been easy. I remember living in San Francisco reading self-help books and perusing dating websites on what I thought was the ultimate quest for love. I shared boldly with friends, family, and anyone else who would listen that love was going to find me in California. Ironically, it was not the historically gay affirming coastal city of San Francisco where I first found love, but a small, quaint college town in Georgia. I thought I was going crazy when it happened. Have you ever had that moment when your eyes and ears are seeing and hearing one thing, but your heart understands something else? If you haven't, trust me, one day, in the not-so-distant future, you will.

While in Georgia, I felt a connection with someone like I had never felt before. My heart, overjoyed and naïve to pain, leapt at the opportunity to invite this new love to experience something magical with me. What I got in response to that invitation was cold, abrupt rejection. At first, I thought perhaps I had misinterpreted, perhaps my heart was wrong, and my ears and eyes had better hearing and vision than my spirit. I thought perhaps the love interest that I had so valiantly pursued was just evil, cruel, and without any regard for me. What the pages of this book chronicle are the truth about the difficulties of finding and accepting love. My heart was not wrong, and the recipient of my love was not laden with evil; he was consumed by pain.

I know what it is like to struggle, to meet others with kindness, and through no fault of your own, to be met with another person's inability to accept acts of love. I know what it is like to have the loves of your life—such as a parent, a soul mate, or in my case, both—call you names, look at you with disdain, and meet your love with full intent not to see it expressed. Beyond the struggle, disappointment, fear, and hurt, my life bears witness to the truth that through it all, you and I have the power to rise above, to excel and succeed despite the acts of others. This book is not a magic pill, and you might have to read it again, and again, to understand all of the many truths it holds. What *The Invitation to Love* will do, though, if you allow it, is to show you a power you did not know possible, to offer you the truth of the dynamic, beautiful person that our Creator intended you and me to be. This book asks you to consider that when people do not speak to your beauty, when people do not attempt to lift you up, what they are doing is not demonstrating your lack of worth, but a testament to their own self-hate.

The pages of this book are not meant to vilify; they are meant to offer you an understanding of forgiveness and love. Forgiveness is simply an accurate viewpoint of a set of events involving another. Forgiveness does not absolve someone of his or her actions, but it notes how fear, pain, shame, and guilt act as conduits for the ineffective practices of others.

I have experienced death, childhood abuse, and bouts of poverty, but nothing I have ever encountered has introduced me to greater pain than the pursuit of love. In Elizabeth Gilbert's bestselling memoir *Eat, Pray, Love*, she recounts stories of people after the Tsunami hit, who had lost everything, and when asked about their lives, what caused them the most grief was love, and its loss. When I first read the book, I was young and immature; I could not fathom that if I had lost everything, love would be the topic that most consumed my thoughts, but now all these years later, I can see exactly how that happens.

Spiritual leader Dr. Juanita Bynum once said, "If you do not understand my pain, you will never understand my praise." That simple yet prolific statement so nicely underscores the book you are about to read. You see, my purpose with this book is to share with you my story of pain, my intent to persevere, and to transform that pain with the promise of prosperity that is on the other side of grief when we have the courage to stay the course. So, I go one step further than Bynum, and I ask that you use this book to reflect on your own chorus line of pain, so like me, you can change the tone of that melody and allow that pain to become your song of praise.

"Love recognizes no barriers.
It jumps hurdles,
leaps fences, penetrates walls to
arrive at its destination full of hope."

— Maya Angelou

The Invitation to Love

Live In Your Truth

Chapter 1

Spiritual Dimensions of Love

Spirit

There is a force inside us that some call intuition, while others refer to it as the inner voice. I define it as Spirit. Spirit is that energy within each of us that, if we sit still and take notice of the world around us, will guide us in the direction we are destined to go. Often, Spirit speaks to us in ways that seem insane, conjure up fear, or breed anxiety. Those feelings referenced are not Spirit, but what can be defined as EGO—EGO, I was once told, is an acronym that stands for Edging *God* Out. God is that force that personifies truth, showcasing the wonder each of us possesses within ourselves—allowing us to recognize others' wonder.

In my own life, I have seen this sense of inner voice play out on many occasions. Professionally, Spirit has guided me on career paths where doors just seemed to open on their own, where opportunity seemed to present itself out of nowhere. When I applied to graduate school for my

Master's and later for my Ph.D. in higher education administration, both times I was rejected from every school I applied to, but one. Each time, I did not take the rejections as failure, but as God giving me clear direction for where my path should take me. With both the Master's and Ph.D., what I have come to realize is that they were not only about learning (in the academic sense), but each also served as a conduit for strengthening my spiritual muscle. When we find courage to take that first step on a spiritual journey, we will find ourselves confronting old hurts, facing the core of our pain, and answering the true calling of forgiveness.

Symbols

I love that, often, when we sit quietly, God will use a sign—a symbol, word, or song—to support us on the pathway to truth. They are a sign from Spirit that we are on the right path or need to change direction. Those who know me best know my love for the number 17. It's not due to a mystical power, or because of numerology that I appreciate this number; rather, I have come to appreciate the number 17 as one of those symbolic markers to remind me of the pathway I am supposed to be on.

I can't explain all the ways that the number 17 is a marker in my life. It marks the day I was born, it just so happens to be the date on which I realized I was supposed to move to Chicago, and the date I realized the call that forgiveness was offering me to answer. The number does not pop up in blatant ways; it comes as a subtle voice in the background of my life. It's typically after the fact that I realize it was present. For me, God moves in the same way; it's often not a loud boom, but a subtle whisper that I hear God speak. I can be in the car, see a school bus with the number 17, and be reminded of something or someone. I can be at work and look at the time and it says 2:17, which reminds me of a happening in my life. As we go through life, we are invited to look for the quiet whispers of truth—symbols: they often come when courage is waning, fatigue has set in, and the temptation to quit is strong.

You Are What You Eat

In a world that moves so counter to the truth, it becomes imperative to be vigilant about what we put into our spiritual bodies. When friends and loved ones are faced with hard times, I have been known to say, "Go sit down in a dark room with a candle lit." While most times this is said in jest, I would be remiss if I did not admit that there are many days when I sit in a metaphorical dark room with a candle lit.

Many days, I am offered advice from all perspectives, some telling me to quit, some telling me to persist, another saying, "Do both—stay and keep your eye out for something better." In the path of love, we all have our varied stories (good and bad) that give us our depiction of what love is and how it should be experienced. So it comes as no surprise that if we ask 100 people to describe love, more than likely we will get 100 different responses. Among such chaos and divergent opinions, it becomes imperative for us to find a way to discern the various voices and extrapolate those of truth.

Personally, I love a good book that can lead me on a pathway of truth. Some of my favorite texts are quoted throughout this work. Good texts, for me, are like food for the soul. I have seen firsthand the positive results that come about in my relationships based on what I am feeding my spirit.

When I seek the counsel of friends who have made vengeance their confidant and anger their ally, I find myself more moved to anger and more willing to attack the position of another. In contrast, when I speak with friends who move with love and follow their own internal compass (Spirit), I find myself more at peace and full of hope. It took years of growth and maturity to get to the place where I can discern from whom to seek counsel. I also make note to spend time with texts that I consider to be words of truth. In the mixture of conversations with like-minded individuals and in vigilant meditation on texts, I find stores of truth; it's in that space that I cultivate the strength to weather life's greatest storms.

Jack & Ennis

L ove is hard; it's hard for various reasons. But deep, soul-churning love invites the participants to move beyond the five senses. In U.S. culture, the term "gay-dar" has been used to reference someone's ability to sense someone's non-heterosexual orientation without the person disclosing it. Love has its own "radar" of sorts that does not rely on the five senses, but instead on that inner voice, Spirit. Let me offer here a deeper perspective of what this looks like in action.

To move beyond the five senses often conjures up fear and doubt. It's like when you ask a friend whom you believe is gay if he is gay; you may feel fear in the inquiry, and even if he says, "No," you still have your own thoughts about the matter. Similarly, love offers the same doubt and questioning. We can often question, using the five senses, whether someone loves us, but the answer cannot rest alone in our taste, sight, touch, smell, and hearing. Rather, we have to go beyond the five senses to that space inherent in each of us.

In the movie *Brokeback Mountain* (which, if you have not seen, I thoroughly recommend), Ennis Del Mar, played by Heath Ledger, and Jack Twist, played by Jake Gyllenhaal, find themselves in a romantic relationship. At the beginning of the movie, Ennis and Jack appear to be two heterosexual ranchers who have been assigned to the same region for work. Early in the film, the two men find themselves sharing a tent; Jack makes a sexual pass at Ennis, which is rejected. Jack makes a pass at Ennis a second time, which Ennis rejects with physical violence. As an audience member, at this point, you think, "When is Jack going to realize his advances are not warranted? Furthermore, how does he even know if this guy is gay?" On the third advance, Ennis fully succumbs to Jack's advances and they have their first sexual encounter.

Upon my first time seeing the film, I was left confused— still questioning how Jack knew to continue his advances when nothing from the five senses was saying his attempts were appropriate. Now, I understand that Jack was not using the five senses for his decision. Rather, Jack had learned the valuable lesson of listening to the voice of the Spirit. Jack felt a connection with Ennis that went beyond the five senses; that connection moved in the spiritual realm where all truth resides. If we are open to it, we are all able to tap into this "spiritual sight." When you look for a life partner, ask yourself whether you are in tune with this person on a spiritual level; can you go without speaking, but know the other person's feelings? Can you hear a song on the radio and feel as though that is a call to action about something in your relationship? All of these are signs of spiritual unity. Look at some of the most famous celebrity couples: Josh Duhamel and Fergie, or Jay-Z and Beyoncé—each couple has noted in interviews their spiritual connections with their partners.

To believe in going beyond the five senses is not based in any particular religious doctrine; it's based in faith. Faith is where deep and soul-churning love is held because faith is the work of the hand of God, and it is within those hands of God that the richest love in life is held.

Chapter 2

Forgiveness

The Great Barrier
to Forgiveness

L ike everyone else, I have experienced the imperfection of humans. And those imperfections have given me moments of pain, disappointment, and sadness. Through each experience, what I have come to realize is that despite the circumstances, I am in 100 percent control of myself and can choose how I react to other people's actions.

It's always interesting to look at the stories we tell each other versus what truly happened. Often, we start the conversation like this: "I had a fight with my partner and decided to pig out on ice cream and watch movies." We make such statements as if the two things are correlated: we had a fight, and thus I decided to eat ice cream—the truth is that the choice to eat ice cream was all our own. It had nothing to do with the other person, but when we link the two together, we undeservedly put the power and responsibility on someone else.

When we place power and responsibility upon another person, we put ourselves in jeopardy—in jeopardy of resentment, anger, and not fulfilling God's great invitation to forgive. Take, for example, your parents divorcing during your first year of college. The devastation is strong, so you decide to quit school. Four years later, you still have not returned and you are in a job with limited opportunities. And then here is where the story begins: You start to say, "If only my parents had not divorced, I could be happy, or I would have finished school, or I would be on a more lucrative career path."

The pathway to forgiveness invites a healing of the soul. In other words, forgiveness results when we come to understand that power should never involuntarily be given to another. In other words, the spirit is indestructible. In my own life, I have experienced the truth of this statement on two occasions.

The first occasion occurred with my dad; my relationship with him was fueled with difficulties that often led me to places of fear and anxiety when I was in his presence. During the final months of earning my Ph.D., I came to realize that my dad could not hurt me any longer—I was no longer a little kid full of vulnerability.

I started to look at those areas of my life where I was not currently living out the fullest expression of myself. For me, the biggest one was in my avoiding all interactions with my dad. At that moment, I understood the power I was giving him. I was giving him the power to control my actions, which was leading to my fear, disconnection, and an inability to forgive. From that day forward, I committed to calling him once a week on Thursdays and visiting him on Sundays—it was hard, and painful at first, but not long after this commitment was made, I began to see a shift in my perception about him. A liberation came about for me, and a new wave of possibility now existed in my relationship with my dad.

The second invitation to heal my soul came during a very vulnerable experience with a friend. Our relationship had hit an impasse, and I was full of disappointment in the breakdown of possibility that had occurred. Like many of us do, I began to blame the other person for the relationship's breakdown. I thought, "If only he did this, or if only he did that." One day, I had the biggest of breakthroughs—I realized the role and responsibility I had in the matter. I realized I would avoid going many places in my town from fear of seeing my former friend and being reminded that our relationship was not where I wanted it to be. My avoidance of him in an effort to stop my pain and fear was actually the life support system that was keeping that pain and fear alive. From that day forward, I intentionally went to neighborhoods I would normally avoid. The first time was hard, but it slowly got easier and easier until the great day came when I felt liberation: when I understood that my power is my own, and only I give permission for others to receive it.

To Completion

I love the question, "How?" It's one of the fundamental questions of life—we ask how to love ourselves, how to find joy, and how to forgive. One of the truths I have found regarding forgiveness is our ability to bring things to completion. It was in the quiet space of meditation that I came to terms with the pattern of forgiveness in my own life. Many times, I have felt called to do certain things, from getting my Ph.D. to writing this book.

In each of those seasons of life, I have been faced with difficulties, many times in my relationships with others. With my father, I found my Ph.D. to be part of the catalyst to forgiveness. For years, I had given my father a level of power that was not his to hold. I regarded my father much of my life with fear, as if he had the power to hurt me. While working in San Francisco, I found myself called to move forward to pursue my Ph.D. When I was finally accepted into a Ph.D. program at the University of Georgia, I was ecstatic. The opportunity to complete a terminal degree at an institution with an academic reputation like Georgia was a gift beyond exciting to me. Soon after starting the Ph.D. process, I came to understand why it's called a "terminal degree." The process of attaining my Ph.D. was truly the most emotionally and spiritually taxing process of my life. The whole way through, I knew I was called to complete the degree. Everything had flowed in such a fashion that I just knew this was a door opening up for me.

About six months before I finished my Ph.D., I felt ready to reach out to my father to reconnect in our relationship. What I realize now, which I did not understand at the time, was that by that point in my educational process, I was in a place where I was confident I would finish. For much of my Ph.D. experience, I had been insecure, feeling vulnerable that any slight hiccup or disturbance in any relationship would send me on a deep spiral downward that I would not be able to get out of, causing me not to complete my degree.

When I realized I would finish my degree, I accepted that all power and influence was under my command. I truly realized, not just cognitively, but also felt in my inner core, that regardless of how my father responded, I would finish this degree. I dislodged my dad from being responsible for my destiny (in this case, my attainment of a Ph.D.).

I explained this realization to a friend in this manner: "Imagine you are getting ready for a road trip from Los Angeles to New York; you are not confident in your driving skills, and at every turn, you feel afraid of what may lie ahead. You have a friend, who is terrible to call on road trips; he constantly makes you feel anxiety when you drive and continually puts you in a place of questioning whether or not you have what it takes to finish the road trip. You decide not to call him for the better part of your journey. Now, you are in New Jersey; you see a sign that says, 'New York 20 miles ahead.' You realize you are almost there, that you are actually going to complete this drive cross-country. At this point, you call your friend, excited to have a conversation, with little care about the nagging that may ensue when he asks you about the gas level in your car, whether you've checked your oil, or the traffic on the large bridges ahead that connect New Jersey and New York. At this point, you could care less how he responds when he answers the phone because you know, regardless of his response, positive or otherwise, you will complete this journey."

In life, we have to listen to that still, quiet voice that is telling us what it is that needs to be complete in our lives. For some, it might be completing one's education. For others, it might be coming to terms with a lifelong journey with weight or body image. It might be a dream you have had for years, but you put it on the back burner because of the ever-present distractions of life. Whatever the case may be, find what needs to be made complete; get about the business of completing those things, so you can be a clearing for strong, loving, and authentic conversations with others— that is where the real power of enacting forgiveness resides.

Thanksgiving

For many of us, old hurts start in our childhood. For me, it was the false sense of rejection I felt when my father left my mother. At the time, I thought my dad's absence was about me. I asked myself, "What is wrong with me? Am I not smart enough? Kind enough?" I was continuously struggling to figure out what I could do differently to win my father's affection.

What I know now is my dad was on his own journey. Being twenty, with a son, would invoke fear in almost anyone—my dad was a victim of fear. I see now that my father did and still does love me. What I experienced then as a child was a man who loved, and loved deeply, but just did not have the ability to show me love in a way I could understand and receive. That's the power of forgiveness, that keen ability to see things not from the perspective of our ego, but from truth and compassion.

One Thanksgiving, I was visiting my half-sister who suf-
fered from the cancer of abandonment by an absent father
as much as I did. That day, her father called her to wish
her a Happy Thanksgiving. The conversation lasted all of
three minutes, and when the telephone call ended, she was
mad, frustrated, and hurt. Her response to me was, "How
can he go for months without talking to me, and then the
first time we talk, he is only on the phone with me for
three minutes?" Her outrage and hurt were obvious, and I
understood since I had been there myself, as have millions
of others. In that moment, rather than going to the place
of sympathy, I said, "Don't you see how hard it must be
for this man to garner the courage to call you and to hear
about your life—a life he is not a part of? That would be
too much for anyone to bear—and I would have responded
the same way, by getting off the phone with you as quickly
as I could."

In that moment, my sister's whole disposition changed,
almost as if she were having an internal dialogue, an "I
never thought of it that way" moment. In an instant, her
tone changed, her feelings toward her father moved from
disdain to compassion, and she was freed of anger. That's
the power of forgiveness; it shares space with the great
gift called liberation. You see, had my sister gone the rest
of the day harboring that pain and resentment, it would

have seeped into her interactions with family, caused her to miss out on the blessing of fellowship, and ruined a holiday rooted in family and tradition.

What I have learned is that hate and anger rob us, not others. Beyond the first love of our father or mother, there are the individuals who try to enter a space of intimacy with us, but because of the holes left by our parent(s), whom we perceive as having left us, these individuals are never able fully to meet our expectations. The question becomes: How could they? We place our advertisement for a lover, but in the job description, we ask for a lover, a confidant, a security granter, a confidence booster, a void filler—because what we fail to acknowledge in the job description for our intimate partner is that what we are looking for is our parent who was never there. Until we go back to the place of hurt and pain, and we address our wounds with our parent(s), dead or alive, we will continue to find ourselves in unfulfilled and dysfunctional relationships, which incite insecurity.

Emancipation

I remember when I first began dating as an adult, I would work out, stress about what to wear, stress about what to say, read books on dating—all trying to get to the place of perfection to woo the heart of another. When a guy would not call, I would call; I would hound him to the point of being overbearing, self-sabotaging what could have been a naturally good moment and potential dating situation because of my "smothering" behaviors. Many times, my pursuits were reciprocated with interest. At those times, I would lose interest, no longer wanting to engage with the person and making up excuses for my behavior, when in actuality, I was not emotionally available myself.

This fear of abandonment resides in so many people, reflected in continuous questioning of our partners, and self-blaming and critiquing until we become a harbor of hate within ourselves. We look to a relationship, or the validation of a man or woman whom we deem cute enough, personable enough, or rich enough, to emancipate us from our hate, when in truth, the only person who holds the key to the prison of loathing we reside in is ourselves.

The Wrong One

We all can fall victim to feelings of anger and frustration. Our partners, friends, and loved ones can often be the targets of our pent-up frustration and anger. As shepherds of love, we continually have to commit ourselves to not mistakenly displacing anger and frustration on those who were never the intended targets of our feelings. Sometimes, we can exhibit this anger at the wrong person and not even know it. One time, I was visiting relatives, a husband and wife. When the husband lost the remote to the television, his wife lost her mind.

She yelled and yelled, lamenting about his consistent lack of responsibility to hold on to things. As she was continuing to yell at her husband, I began to conclude that her anger was a lot greater than warranted by a missing television remote. When she had cooled off a bit, I asked her about her anger toward her husband, and she vented again about the missing remote. I then asked her whether she had ever considered perhaps her anger was misplaced. She questioned me, befuddled by my query. Knowing her well, I offered perhaps the anger she was directing toward her husband was really the anger she held toward her father—a parent who for many years had been neglectful in his care. After taking some time to consider this possibility, she realized that her father was the source of much of her frustration that she directed at her husband, and only by mending her relationship with her father could she authentically communicate her feelings to her husband.

Far too often, we do not take enough time to reflect and give consideration to our behavior and how it might have its roots in more than our current circumstances. If you are the object of others' frustration, then as Don Miguel Ruiz sums it up in his book, *The Four Agreements*, do not take others' actions personally. To those who perpetuate their anger and frustration onto others: consider the situation, your past experiences, and then determine whether your frustration is being directed at the wrong person.

Man's Best Friend

I was watching Animal Planet's *Pit Bulls and Parolees*. The show is based on a family who has committed their lives to rescuing dogs, rehabilitating them, and finding them safe and loving homes. This particular episode featured a man who was moving, so he was dropping a dog off at the shelter. The dog, upon his arrival, appeared to be malnourished and clearly from a neglectful home. The dog's owner, full of shame and guilt, initially claimed the dog belonged to someone else and he was doing a favor for a friend.

As the man was driving off, the dog whimpered and watched with sadness. The dog's expression clearly acknowledged that the man was his owner and not just a good Samaritan doing a favor for a friend. I was moved that, despite the neglect the dog had experienced, he still watched his owner with loving eyes, to the point of grieving when his owner drove away.

I suppose that is why dogs are called man's best friend. Dogs are one of the greatest examples of unconditional love—looking with an eye of goodness we, as humans, are limited in our ability to see with. I believe some would call that grace. Grace is a space we should all strive to attain——the place where we can see the good in others despite their faults.

I am not suggesting we should permit others to treat us poorly. Case in point, the dog did not stay with the owner, nor did the rescuers try to discourage the owner from leaving the dog behind. Both parties knew the owner had no capacity to care for an animal. What I offer, rather, is encouragement in knowing if a dog, which has been mistreated, neglected, and abandoned, can find a space for grace, then we, as humans, should be able to muster up the might to do the same for one another.

Chapter 3
The Love Within

The Self-Love Test

As we begin to develop intimate relationships with others, the first thing we want to do is ascertain their level of self-love. But how? The test for evaluating someone else's self-love is simple. Here are two examples: If your love interest is someone who over-indulges in spending, in eating, or in recreational drug use, those are all clear-cut examples of another's self-love tank not being full. If you are gay, and your love interest is not out of the closet, that is another surefire way of becoming aware that his or her self-love tank is not full. I am not advising you not to pursue a relationship with these individuals; rather, I posit it would be good to consider these things in regards to your expectations for them to be able to fully show you love in return.

To illustrate this point, I am going to personify two inanimate objects. The first illustration involves a treadmill. A person can have a strong desire to run on a treadmill, even speak of running on a treadmill all day long, but until he actually gets on the treadmill, his words are just thoughts with no action. A person can have strong love for you, speak of you often, and hold you in the highest regard, with a strong desire to present herself well in your life, but without self-love, her words just become thoughts without action. When this happens, we question her love for us. This is wrong, and it leaves us confused because what we should be questioning is not the person's love, but her effectiveness in expressing love. You see, those with high levels of self-love take responsibility for their lives, responsibility for their relationships, and allow their love for themselves to show through. A person who wants to lose weight and loves herself, not only talks about getting on the treadmill, but goes one step further and actually gets on it for a run.

If you experience someone whose self-love tank is low, I offer this illustration for you. Imagine a person has ten million dollars in the bank, but until he is able to take responsibility for his life and withdraw money from the ATM machine, his wallet will be empty and he will perceive himself as poor, even though his bank account has plenty of wealth. In this illustration, you are the ATM and your partner is the person with the million dollar bank account. In short, when your partner shows up for you as "poor" with a wallet that seems empty, it is your opportunity to show love for yourself by responding to him, not as the poor person he sees himself as, but as the millionaire he is. Through your response to people's poor behavior, people begin to see the different possibilities for how they can show up in others' lives and in their own. This act of seeing the millionaire behind the pauper exterior is hard, so sometimes, we have to remove ourselves from the environment to give ourselves time for reflection before we can respond appropriately. When people show up as "poor" and we call them "poor," all we do is reinforce the long-standing belief they already hold about themselves. The miracle of loving someone else is the opportunity to grow in our own self-love as we begin to demonstrate love effectively to others.

Love the One You're With

The popular saying goes, "If you can't be with the one you love, love the one you're with." I have practiced this saying so much, and boy, have I learned the consequences of not mastering this concept in my own life. When a relationship did not work, I would be on to the next, looking for the next person to release my pain, ease my anxiety that I was unattractive, and be my source of joy. With each pursuit, I found myself ultimately unsatisfied, void, and losing a bit of the essence of who I am. It's like being hungry and eating a bag of potato chips, or being thirsty and going for a sugary drink. Sure, the chips satisfy the hunger, and yes, the drink will satisfy thirst, but the long-term results from engaging in both too often will leave you unhealthy and unfulfilled.

I am not arguing that you shouldn't "love the one you're with." I am simply reframing and offering perhaps the one you are with is yourself. For me, loving the one you're with meant noticing the invitations that were coming to me. I would have friends invite me to dinner, but because they were not potential suitors, I would turn them down, or be in haste to leave so I could hit the bar or another environment where a potential suitor might be found. I would reject love from dogs, cats, fish, and humans alike, all because none of them was the one I felt could fulfill my need. What I wanted was someone who was attractive, who made me feel worthy, who gave me everything I was not giving myself.... What I got in that pursuit was junk food. The junk food of rejection, the junk food of superficial relationships, the junk food of interactions that engaged my five senses but did nothing to stimulate my soul.

Like my friends who love sugary pop drinks or bags of potato chips, I still have cravings. The temptation to engage in ways counter to my truth (often based on my fear of being alone) is beyond difficult to manage at times. As I grow into who I am, I run less often to the nearest person who can fulfill my emotional hunger. Instead, I pause, love the one I am with, and find those healthier options in whatever form: a dog, cat, fish, or other humans who allow for the holistic celebration of the greatest lover I will ever have: me.

I Can Treat You No Better
Than I Treat Myself

S o many times in my life, I have looked at people and wondered why they treated me so poorly. Why, with all the love I attempted to share, couldn't they find a way to show me the same love in return? These questions were all answered when I came to understand one truth: people cannot treat me any better than they treat themselves. One time in particular, I had a loved one whom I was at a considerable impasse with. I went to his home and saw dishes piled in the sink, that his routine meals consisted of junk food and sweets, and all his other meals were takeout. My friend treated himself like crap. I saw firsthand then that people can treat us no better than they treat themselves. Next time you want an assessment of how someone is going to treat you, look at the way he keeps his home, look at his relationship to healthy living, look at his relationship with money, and look at his relationship with himself, that is, his level of self-acceptance. Once you have looked at those things in their totality, you then will be able to get a sense of how he will treat you.

The Fab Five

I have often griped to friends and loved ones about the challenges I have faced in dating, or in relationships in general. In these situations, I have usually put responsibility on the other person for why things were not working. Long, long, ago, however, I realized that I have to take responsibility for the role I play in a relationship. Even with that understanding, I did not know how to manifest it in my day-to-day life, especially when it came to dating.

One day, I sat down and started to look back on all of my previous dating experiences that had not worked out well. I looked for patterns to see what were the common links between them. I came up with a list of five things that when combined are strong indicators that a relationship will not work well for me.

For me, a relationship is not limited to dating; it is a broad term used to define any dedicated time I spend forging a bond with someone. The "Fab Five," as I like to refer to them, include: a person's relationship with him- or herself, a person's relationship with his or her parents, a person's relationship with money, a person's relationship with his or her home, and a person's relationship with food.

A Person's Relationship with Him- or Herself

We have all met people, at one time or another, who in one circumstance or environment, act one way (e.g., on social media), and in a different space, are entirely different people. I have seen that when a person's expression is influenced more by his/her environment and less by who he/she is authentically, it is a great sign that he/she has not fully cultivated an appreciation of who he/she is, and thus, the probability exists he/she will not be able to cultivate a full appreciation for me.

A Person's Relationship with His or Her Parents

I know firsthand how ineffective I was in my relationships with other people because of my inability to forgive my father and forge a healthier relationship with him. While we cannot all have happy, loving relationships with our parents, for a host of reasons that may be beyond our responsibility and power to manage, each of us can make peace with those relationships. I have seen people make peace with parents who are dead, with parents who are verbally and physically abusive, and with parents who are addicted to substances to ease their own pain. While the process is difficult, the path to forging an honest and healthy relationship with our parents (living or deceased) is not only possible, but also pertinent to forging healthy relationships with others.

A Person's Relationship with Money

I treated money like it was water, used it up, until the well was dry, not thinking of long-term impact, or of how it would affect my future. Similarly, I would run my own well dry, working harder and harder, being more and more self-critical, trying to buy myself proof I was enough. I used money to manifest this need for being enough: buying clothes and other goods that expressed my attractiveness or showed my social stature, all in a vain, superficial attempt to garner connection and love. Just as I did not understand money's true purpose, I did not see my own true purpose. It was not until I redefined my relationship with money I could begin the process of redefining the relationship I had with myself.

A Person's Relationship with Food

Our relationship with food is so much bigger than what we eat. How we use food reflects the beauty, or lack thereof, we see within ourselves. I had a friend I would talk to almost daily, sharing stories of our day and the happenings in our lives. I would start the conversations with small talk, such as, "How was your day?" or "What did you have for lunch?" Over time, I realized every time he talked about what he had to eat for the day, it was often next to nothing. He would speak of working long hours at his job, with high expectations for output, so he would grab a cookie for lunch, or a candy bar for breakfast, and then have a doughnut for dinner. The first time he talked about his eating habits, I chalked it up to him having a busy day, but soon, I saw it was a pattern. Then I realized the junk food he was putting in his body reflected the "spiritual junk" he would say about himself. He did not see himself as great, and thus, he did not put great things in his body. When our relationship with food is crap, it is often a sign we see ourselves as crap; if we see ourselves as crap, how can we show up as anything other than crap for those we love the most?

A Person's Relationship with His or Her Home

My mom once shared with me her friend's inability to appreciate her. My mom would do all she could to support her friend, but her friend would be unable to recognize all the ways my mom was attempting to demonstrate love. My mother chalked up her friend's behavior simply to being ungrateful. Then one day, my mom's friend got sick, so she asked my mom to come over and help her care for her house. The house was a mess. My mom was so surprised to see the state of her friend's home; it was her first time seeing it, but soon after she got there, she realized it was the home's natural state. At that moment, all of the grief my mother had shared about her friend made sense to me. When she shared this experience with me, I said to my mom, "How can your friend fully acknowledge the care you show to her, when she is unable to show care for herself, as evident in the way she cares for her home?"

I do not share the Fab Five to promote shame or guilt. We all fall into these patterns...many of us have bounced a check, gone through a drive-thru for a burger instead of eating a salad at home, had dirty plates and laundry distributed around our house, had an impasse with a parent, and shown up as less than fully authentic under various circumstances. However, when the Fab Five are not executed in combination in a healthy manner, on a regular basis, not becoming part of our habitual ways of being, then we compromise the full expression of our love for others, and the love they hope to express to us.

Chapter 4
Fear in Love

Protect Themselves

For years, I thought people told lies to protect others. For example, I am not going to tell Jane, because it would hurt her, or I am not going to tell Bob, because I don't want to stress him out. Truth be told, we do not lie to protect other people; we lie to protect ourselves. Only when we accept this fact can we get to the truth, the marrow of why we lie to others.

If you catch someone in a lie, you may question the person's love or regard for you and whether his or her intent comes with a true spirit of goodwill. I offer it is fear, the antithesis of love, that causes people to lie. The greater you love someone, the more your fear may build for a potential rejection down the road. In those cases, we lie to protect ourselves and build a false sense of security in the relationship. Since love and fear can't reside at the same time, if fear prevails, a lie is told.

When people lie, it is not because they are necessarily bad or have bad intentions; the lie is just a declaration that they have decided to side with fear because love was too big a risk to take.

Dismantling Fear

I once heard thought and spiritual leader Esther Hicks say whenever we are experiencing fear, it is an indication we are not yet ready to manifest those things that are part of our destiny. "Fear," with perhaps the exception of "love," is the most referenced word throughout this book, which makes sense, because our only barrier to love is fear.

I spent a number of years living in a prolonged state of fear, which is often referred to as "suffering." To move past my suffering, I read books, meditated, and sought wise counsel, but with each activity, the fear remained. Then one day, as I drove to work, I had an epiphany—the way to dismantle fear is to do those things I want to do.

Here's a tangible example: Let's say you love going to the park and spending days walking the trails and seeing nature. However, you have a strong fear of bees and allow your fear of bees to keep you from the park you love to visit. At that moment, you have offered power to the bees, and every time your desire to go to the park kicks in, you allow the fear of bees to keep you from going, you are creating larger spaces of fear, and decreasing levels of love (in this case, your love for the park).

In my own life, I have experienced metaphorical times of sacrifice I thought were leading me closer to my destiny, but in reality, they were pulling me further away from it. I thought to live in my truth meant to sacrifice those things I wanted to do, in order to manifest the things I desired to have. With each sacrifice, what I was doing was actually increasing fear, which led to greater levels of resentment. I would think about what I wanted to manifest, such as long-term love and kids. But I thought the way to manifest those things was to avoid scenes I did not think could provide those goals; for example, I would avoid going out to bars with friends, thinking, "Love is not found there, so why even bother going?" The challenge, though, was I had a desire to go out with my friends; I enjoyed gathering socially over a good drink and dancing. What I could not reconcile was that I was not ready to manifest what my heart desired, and furthermore, make peace with not being ready.

I thought to do those things I enjoyed would only defer my destiny. In truth, I was not really in a space to settle down, experience long-term love, and have a family. If I had been really ready to manifest my destiny, those things—going out with friends to bars and dancing on the weekends—would not be seen as obstacles to my heart's desires. I had to emancipate myself from self-imposed restraints, explore, and move beyond sacrifice so I could authentically arrive at the place where I was emotionally and mentally mature enough to handle love.

Whether it is going to the park despite bees, or going out with friends despite long-term desires to have a family and be at home on the weekends, we must each ascertain what sacrifices we are making that are limiting joy and exacerbating fear. We can find peace in knowing our destiny is not deferred by doing those things we enjoy. As long as we express love to ourselves, and love to others, what is destined for us will never be denied.

Water-Based Fruits

I remember the summer after finishing my Ph.D., I decided I was going to grow a garden, a garden of water-based fruits: tomatoes, cucumbers, and strawberries. I was so excited about my gardening adventure. I went to the plant store and got all my supplies, watered my fledgling plants, and shared pictures of my new adventure via social media. Then life happened. With trips galore planned over the summer, my attention to my garden became less consistent; weeks would go by without me caring for my plants. By August, I was seeing the consequence of my inability to be attentive and consistent in my care of my garden. By the year's end, I understood how my gardening experience was teaching me lessons for other areas of my life, such as love and its correlation to fear.

My behavior in expressing love at times has been like my gardening: anything but consistent. Some days, I was like a gardener watering the plants of love often; other times, when life served up distractions or the "fruits" of the relationship were not yielding as I would like, I would shut down, withdraw, and become the antithesis of what it means to express love effectively.

The truth I have begun to understand is that consistent behavior supports the dissolution of fear. In other words, our consistent practice of expressing love effectively serves as the best conduit to release the fear of love within another. Sometimes, that may mean giving space to a partner or a child who is grappling with the terms of the relationship. In other cases, it is being a sustained presence to demonstrate your commitment. Love's expression varies, is situational, and is best demonstrated by the direct communication and request of the other party in the relationship. If the other person is in tune to being in love with himself or herself, he/she will be able to tell you directly how best to show love. In the case where people can't give you clear understanding of how best to express love to them, two things are probable: they don't know the answer themselves, or life is offering you the opportunity to sit still and listen to your own internal compass for guidance. With my garden, I could not control the weather, when it rained, or whether pests would stay away; similarly, with love, I cannot control another person's actions, ability to accept love, or give it in return. With both my garden and the love I seek to express, I have full control of my consistent practice of engaging in acts that support the growth of my plants and relationships.

The Big Bad Wolf

G rowing up, I had an image of my father that was less than flattering. My father and mother met during their college years. Neither was ready to be a parent, but in a space not cultivated by love, but by the desires and actions of young adulthood, I was conceived. My mother assumed many of the responsibilities in raising me, while my father moved back to New Jersey, an eight-hour drive from our home in North Carolina. Over the years, my opinion of my father diminished. I saw him as someone who acted inconsistently, and who often fell through on promises made.

Then when I was eleven, I went to live with my father for a year. That year was difficult since I was a preteen getting to know a parent for the first time. I remember one day in particular when we had a conflict. That day, I was going to fly back to North Carolina to visit my mom; I was rushing, and my dad began to yell at me to hurry down the stairs, fearing

I would miss my flight. When I got in the car, I accidentally stained the seat of his car with fresh paint that had come off the wall as I was carrying my bag down the stairs. I will never forget my father's anger in that moment. He yelled, cursed, said he was tired of seeing my face, and he was glad he would not see it anymore—he used a couple of other expletives, but the spirit of what was said is here. I remember saying to myself, "God, if you get me out of here, he will never have to worry about seeing my face again." He didn't see my face either, for another seven years until I graduated from high school. We went years without speaking. After I completed high school, my dad and I continued to have a tense relationship; he missed my college graduation and other opportunities to reconnect with me, which continually led me to believe he was a bad person.

Then one day when I was in graduate school, pursuing my Ph.D., I was on the phone with my dad—we had not talked in months. Like my father often did, he started the conversation critically, using the conversation as an opportunity to give me "constructive feedback." Later that afternoon, I went to his home and shared with him how our conversations made me feel. I told him that when he spoke to me in a critical way, because we did not have much of a relationship for context, I could not help but think he was rude, and I knew he did not want me to feel that way about him. As

I spoke, I could see the look on his face begin to change. I could see pain in his face, and he then shared that he felt so upset that he almost wanted to jump off the roof to end it all. At that moment, I began to realize my father was not a monster, not the big bad wolf I had made him out to be. Rather, my father, like many people, is someone who has experienced bouts of pain. That moment was a cosmic shift in my own understanding; I gained awareness and now understood that what I had once thought was evil in him was just a manifestation of pain.

Thus, on that day, began a slow and steady shift toward forgiveness of my father. I began little by little to see who he was beyond the stories I had crafted about him. I began to see him less as Satan and more as a savior. You see, my poor relationship with my father was having a domino effect on my ability to connect intimately with others—something I desperately wanted. I realized for me to open up space for new possibilities for love, I first had to open up new possibilities in my ties with my father.

Foster Child Theory

I love a good metaphor, and I am frequently apt to use one to explain a concept that seems complex. The question often arises, "How can I show someone so much love, yet in return, experience cold and disconnection?" My theory does not explain everything, but it comes with the promise of large applicability to solve this issue. I call this one "The Foster Child Theory."

Think of a child who is in the foster care system whose experience is muddled with abuse and neglect. The child is finally placed in a loving and well-resourced home; this experience is foreign to the child, so while a child from a loving upbringing might look to his new family with appreciation and love, this child is reserved, outwardly unappreciative, and hesitant in his willingness to show love—the child is guarded, thinking, "Let me prepare myself for the inevitable day when my new family no longer wants me; if I am prepared for it, perhaps it will not hurt so bad."

Where it may appear the child does not care, has no love, nor appreciation, in truth, he fears to show his full care, love, and appreciation because if he does and he is then rejected, it would cause him more hurt than he could bear.

This metaphor holds true in love when one partner feels inadequate, and the other person questions the love. What really should be questioned is the other person's sense of self-worth. The guarded partner can be in a relationship with potential for love, in a space with another individual who inspires and cherishes him or her—this experience can be frightening and provoke a guarded nature… one where the partner is waiting and anticipating rejection.

If you are the recipient of this kind of behavior, rather than sit and ponder why your loved one behaves the way he/she does, take a moment to garner your own worth and think, "Wow, how great I must be for this person to hold me in such regard it invokes heightened emotion; while not effective, it is, nonetheless, a testament of his/her perception of me."

Assess your relationship: How does it stack up to the Foster Child Theory? Then remain cognizant of that comparison as you accept the invitation to be in relationships with others. Take note: Love is a commitment, not a feeling, and sometimes difficulty, trial, and testing is the only real measure and expression of how love is realized.

Fried Fish Fridays at Grandma's

When I was younger, I would love going to my grandmother's house on the weekends. You see, every Friday she would fry fish, and to me, her fish were the best in the world. I would eat my grandmother's fish smiling from ear-to-ear, elated by the taste of the salty and savory meal.

My grandmother's fish reminds me a lot of love. For me, the enjoyment I displayed eating her food had nothing to do with her; it was my authentic expression based on the joy I received from experiencing her cooking. As a young child, I could not tell Grandma that it was the mix of seasoned salt and cornmeal batter that made me love her fish, or the way she used peanut oil instead of vegetable oil, or that she mainly fried flounder rather than trout or another type of fish—all I knew was I loved its taste and the feeling I received from eating it.

Love in its purest sense is the same. We can't always articulate what is the "seasoning" or "flavor" someone else displays that makes us love being with him or her. Our sense of joy, the light in our eyes, the way we speak of the person, is not for his or her benefit, but it results from our ability to be free and fully expressed in our relationship.

With my grandmother, I felt safe, secure, and loved in that space. I felt comfortable showing up authentically, grinning from ear to ear at the smell and taste of her cooking. If my grandmother had been someone who was abusive, someone I was scared would hurt me, someone whom I felt would abandon me, then my response may have been different. I would have still loved going to Grandma's for fish; I would have still loved the smell of her cooking, and the taste would have still been out of this world, but because of my fear of anticipated neglect, abuse, and abandonment, my reaction might have been different.

Rather than smile from ear to ear, I would have said a simple, "Thanks," flatly, with no excitement. I would have held back my smile; I would have held back my excitement because to express myself fully would have left me vulnerable and susceptible to being hurt by my grandmother. Had my reaction been the latter, my grandmother would have potentially questioned her fish, questioned her cooking in general, and/or questioned my love for her, when really, what would have needed to be questioned was why she inspired a fear that did not allow my love to be fully expressed.

In our lives, we will meet people who will experience us the way I experienced fish on Fridays at Grandma's; that is, they will feel excitement, delight, and enjoyment from the experience. The difference is some people will allow that to be fully expressed, while others, imprisoned by their guards of fear, will not allow their authentic feelings to shine through. As people who want to nurture greatness in others, we continually have to question whether we are experiencing the authenticity of another, or the blankets of doubt, fear, and mistrust that hinder another from full expression.

Self-Expression

E arlier, I spoke of the self-love test. I suppose in some ways this discussion is the second iteration of that conversation. I have come to understand love, and love's expression, are two separate entities. Meaning, I can have deep love for another person, but my ability to express that love is completely separate from the volume of love I possess. Beyond that, what I have come to understand is our ability to express love effectively to another person is directly related to our ability to express love effectively to ourselves.

I remember having drinks with a friend; he would say the most disparaging things about himself—his language was full of hate, and I was taken aback by his self-critique. For years, I had struggled with this friendship, not knowing how to be supportive. That day, at dinner, I saw firsthand that the friendship would continue to struggle until there was a paradigm shift in the way my friend was able to express love for himself.

Our inability to express love for ourselves can take many forms: the way we talk about ourselves, the way we experience food, using sex to self-medicate, consuming drugs and alcohol to mask pain, our willingness to engage in gossip about others, our willingness or unwillingness to date people who are similar to ourselves—perhaps based in race, social economic status, or body type. All of these factors can be indicators of our ability or inability to express love effectively toward ourselves. In short, self-love has a twin named self-acceptance.

Our heart is our greatest treasure, and those we entrust with that treasure are asked to be responsible stewards of it. Just as we ask others to act responsibly when we give them our heart, so too, we are asked to act responsibly in our giving of that treasure. As I move forward now, I keenly watch how others express love toward themselves; I take stock of that expression, and I use it to inform my understanding of their ability and readiness to express love for me.

Taste the Rainbow

L ove is like Skittles; it comes in various varieties and flavors. Often, love is considered a universal thing that manifests itself and is experienced in the same manner by everyone. Over time, I have learned that this view is far from accurate. To the contrary, love comes with a unique composite that is individualized and experienced differently by each person. In the last story, I mentioned that if people cannot effectively love themselves, it makes it difficult for them to express love to others.

While the point is true, it can bear some clarification. First, we must acknowledge love is experienced differently from one individual to the next. Furthermore, I can be highly expressive and effective in my love for one person, while ineffective or at times unwilling to express my love for someone else. Love between two people calls upon different emotions, actions, and spaces. For example, a family member of mine has gone five years without speaking to his daughter, but he talks to his neighbor almost daily. Now, does that mean he loves his neighbor more than his daughter? No, it means the love he shares for his daughter and his ability/willingness to express that love is different than it is for his neighbor.

We can find ourselves in an intimate relationship, questioning someone else's actions, inability to show us love, and overall behavior. We then compare that to how he/she treats other people, questioning, "Why is he/she so nice to this person, or why can he/she show up so effectively in this case, but not with me?" The answer is simple: Love is a personalized phenomenon that can't be quantified through comparison of one relationship to another. A person's way of being with you does not predict how he/she will be with another—it's all part of the individual's journey toward full self-expression, with you as one of his/her teachers.

Theodore Roosevelt once said, "Comparison is the thief of joy." Before we begin the pain-filled journey of comparison, remember love is not the same—like Skittles, it comes with various flavors, each meant to satisfy in different ways. We begin to break through the clouds of pain and inner turmoil only when we recognize and taste the rainbow of love.

Silence Is Golden

St. Augustine said, "Truth is like a lion; you don't have to defend it; let it loose and it will defend itself." Often when we experience others behaving ineffectively, our natural inclination is to vent to friends and loved ones, to share our story of struggle in an effort to attain sympathy and support.

I have found in those moments of venting, I, subconsciously (and sometimes consciously), am persecuting someone else's character. At the time, I thought my actions were justified, but as I have gotten older, that quick need to react is sometimes to the detriment of truth emerging.

You can always reframe how you see a situation—I now understand in the ineffective moments of my relationships, what I am experiencing is not the product, but the process. Put another way, when people show up ineffectively, you are experiencing their pain or fear, instead of who they really are. We speak to this pain or fear as if it truly represented the other person, and through our sharing with and venting to others, what we are doing is passing on permission for the other person to be judged as such by others. To be clear, I do not offer this reframing process as a way to hide others' wrongdoings or make poor behavior permissible; I offer it for consideration about how we share our disappointments with others.

Maya Angelou once said, "When people show you who they are, believe them." I love this quote, but the challenge is people rarely show you who they really are—they show their fear, pain, and insecurity, but those are not attributes of who they are; rather, they are byproducts of the stage of life they are experiencing.

Silence is golden; rather than vent and lament about others' ineffectiveness, do nothing in deed and in word and allow the truth to reveal itself on its own.

Do Nothing

One of the fundamental principles in the book *A Course in Miracles* is that we need not do anything to allow love to emerge. So often in relationships, we feel we need to be taking action, and we ask questions like, "What do I need to do?" or "How do I keep this relationship going?" Sometimes, the answer is to do nothing; to do nothing is to make our ultimate alliance with faith. Recently, I had a friend who was distraught after seeing her relationship with her significant other come to an end. When I spoke to her on the phone, she asked me what she should do to fix the situation. I simply responded, "Do nothing."

Sometimes, love is like a coming out process for someone who is closeted about his or her sexual orientation. Often, when a person is not "out," that person's decision to remain in the closet is based in shame, guilt, and/or fear. At the present time, being gay is an identity the person feels uncomfortable and internally conflicted with. When you ask a person who is closeted, "Are you gay?" nine times out of ten, his response will be an emphatic, "No." The more you press the issue, the more the person will become resentful to the point where he may avoid you altogether, overcome by the continuous pressure to explore his identity. In the same way, love is a coming out process. Conversely, when you allow someone simply to be, often, over time, authentic expressions are presented, and trust is built to allow truth to emerge.

Love moves in the same way; it can invoke fear, inadequacy, and insecurity. When a person is navigating the journey of love, like other forms of coming out, the best way to respond is to be supportive and allow the person just to be, let trust grow over time, do nothing, and let him come out at his own pace. If you are constantly "doing" in a relationship, and you are finding yourself unsatisfied or insecure about the current state of your relationships, consider trying something new: Do nothing—remember, love liberates, and time will bring all things to light.

Chapter 5

Scar Tissue

Genesis

Oftentimes the reason for our ineffectiveness in expressing love is based in our childhood experiences. I was well past thirty when I realized that every person I had ever met who struggled with his or her ability to show and receive love derived that struggle from deep-rooted childhood emotional scars. I was just as much a perpetrator as I was a victim in my inability to express and receive love effectively. Like those around me, I had allowed the scar tissue from childhood hurts to close me off to love.

One time, a dear friend and I committed to supporting each other in waking up early to work out—she would call me, and I would call her. From the beginning, I was nervous about the workout schedule; when we were not able to keep the agreement, I immediately decided it was not working and I wanted to quit. My friend stayed committed to the agreement and said she would continue to call me to sustain her accountability to me.

One morning, in a deep sleep, I missed her call. She called me twice more and left me a voicemail. In a space of frustration, I called her, upset that she had phoned me three times in a row and feeling coerced into keeping an agreement I had already acknowledged was not working for me. My tone was cold, upset, and distant.

Later that afternoon, I reflected on our conversation and how it must have felt for her. I called my friend again, and during our conversation, I realized I was projecting onto her my feelings from having been abused as a child. During the abuse, I felt the assailant had coerced me into the experience and then taken advantage of me—a full loss of power. I realized I was placing on my friend that same feeling of being taken advantage of, seeing her as coercing me in the way I had been coerced as a child. None of my thoughts about my friend were true; on the contrary, they were made up from beliefs based in unhealed pain from my past.

What my friend was offering was love; what I responded with was anything but love. I closed my heart to her in an instant. When I understood how I was using the scars of the past to block love in the present, I was introduced to the universal truth about the genesis of my limitations in experiencing love. I got a glimpse firsthand that we don't need to know someone's childhood story to understand a person's childhood pain. All we have to do is look at the way someone expresses love in the present to understand the unhealed wounds of that person's past.

Helen Keller

So often in life, we notice others' ineffectiveness. We say to ourselves, "If she would just do this, or if she would just do that…just look at how much greater her life would be." We confront friends and loved ones; we find the words, we say them with love, and to our dismay, the recipient is unable to receive or put into practice what we say. We get mad and frustrated, thinking, "Why doesn't she get it?"

What we fail to realize is that we can't verbally communicate with Helen Keller. When people are experiencing dysfunction in their own lives and are on a course full of mistakes, their pain can make them spiritually and emotionally deaf to the truth and love we are trying to convey. As hard as it can be, all we can do is be an example for people, model the way, and liberate them with the prayerful hope that life's classroom will give them the message they so desperately need to hear.

The Gift We Give in Goodbye

S ometimes, there are no better teachers than youngsters to instruct us in lessons on love. My youngest nephew, Micah, has not fallen short in teaching me about love— he loves Uncle Darren and Uncle Darren loves him. Micah, like many four year olds, does not have the strongest communication skills. Many days when he is frustrated or upset, he will revert back to toddler behavior and cry to express his frustration, rather than talk it out as I often would like him to do.

Most days, I can hang in there with Micah when he starts crying. I can coach him through it, provide him support, and show love until his crying spell has passed. Other days, though, when my tolerance for crying has waned, I have come to understand the gift we sometimes give when we say, "Goodbye." Micah, when he is having a really bad moment, can cry and yell with a force to rival most, and some days, I must be honest, it can try my patience. I can find myself frustrated and at the brink of losing it. I want to yell and tell him to stop crying, and boy, the names I conjure up in my head to call him; well, let's just say they are not names fitting for a bright, wonderful child like Micah. In those moments when all my patience has waned, I have had to learn the power of walking away.

The power to walk away is my expression of my love for my nephew and myself. You see, I know that Micah thinks the world of his Uncle Darren. I appreciate and hold that truth with great value; the admiration my young nephew has for me is something I treasure. Because of the love I have for myself, I am not going to allow myself, in a moment of anger and frustration, to let my words and acts compromise the way my nephew looks at me. Rather than respond to my nephew's outburst, at those extreme times, I quietly and gently walk away. I go to another room, I sit to restore my patience, to seek clarity in the situation (in this case an understanding of why he is so upset), and in the meantime, I pray that he is figuring out a better way to communicate with me instead of crying and screaming.

I have also found parallels to my relationship with my nephew in my adult relationships. I have found myself at times frustrated at people who, in my view, do not live up to their full potential. For years, I thought the best thing for me to do in these situations was to stick it out with people, stand beside them, and support them as they grow. While I still agree with my earlier thoughts, I now know that dedication has to be mixed with self-awareness of our own limitations. As with Micah, in many relationships, if I stick around too long, I begin to become part of the problem rather than the solution. I stunt growth rather than being a support to allow it to happen. Now, when I hit those pinnacle points of frustration and resentment, I ask myself, "Is change happening by my continuing to stay here, or am I at the brink of using my words and actions to harm another?"

The gift of goodbye is not saying we are leaving people; rather it is our humble acknowledgment that in this current space, we do not have the capacity to continue to support them. We pray for patience for ourselves, and for others; we pray our departure from the environment provides the impetus and space needed for their growth and the actualization of their potential.

School Is in Session

I n the school of life, people show up to class when they are ready to attend. Not a moment sooner, and not a moment that is in anyone else's control but theirs. When I learned that great truth—that I could not change other people—the change that occurred in me was huge. Now, I had heard most of my adult life that I could not change other people. I would have experiences, though, that led me to the arrogant belief that I could; after all, I would have people tell me how I inspired them, or because of something I did, now they were making changes in their lives. I thought, "If I could be an agent of influence in this person's life, why couldn't I be that same agent of influence for some of the people I love the most."

Then, I got hold of the egotism I was carrying by thinking I was the master architect of people's own growth. To the contrary, people around me who were inspired by my actions had already done the work so they were prepared to make change happen in their lives; I had just been the conduit to help them manifest something already within themselves. There is a big moment, when we discern the difference between people who are already in the class of life to learn and are ready to grow, and those who are full of resistance to live out their truth. We can say the best words and communicate with the highest levels of expression possible, but if people are not prepared and ready to go to class, then the whole session is in vain.

So now, when people close to me, whom I want to see bring about greater possibility in their lives, don't seem to want to show up for the course, I think to myself, "What classroom are they inviting me to?" Many times, when people were not moving in the direction I wanted them to, I would come across as cold and non-responsive, and I would say to myself, " I don't approve of their actions, so to respond to their communication, to engage with them, to show love, is condoning their behavior." I understand now, that each of those opportunities is life putting me in a classroom where I can be loving, caring, and empathetic to another's journey. Life is putting me where I can learn so I'm prepared for the next great classroom that lies ahead.

Note, I am not saying that I invite myself to be in space with people who are not moving in the same direction as me. To the contrary, what I have found is that when I invite situations upon myself, no matter how loving my intention, I put myself in a space of vulnerability where I can cause harm to myself or others. Now, when I am offered the invitation, generated by someone else, I accept it. I seize that moment to show love, empathy, and compassion. I accept invitations sometimes full of fear, not knowing how I will show up with others, but I know God would not give me anything to do that I was not ready to handle.

For example, when my dad and I first started the journey to bring our relationship to a new frontier, he invited me to his home for Thanksgiving. Although at first reluctant, I finally accepted the invitation, knowing those three things (love, empathy, and compassion) were what I was being asked to showcase. The drive to his house was so hard; I had to pull over on the side of the road to call a friend for support—I did not think I had the capacity to be in a space with my dad where he would not cause me harm, and at the same time, I would not cause him harm. However, the visit turned out to be perfect, exactly what I needed it to be, and I demonstrated a strength I did not know possible. All this happened because I did not initiate the invitation. Now, had I initiated the idea of joining my dad for Thanksgiving, the outcome could have been different.... I have seen many times where my intentions were good, but trying to control or change the situation by inserting myself, instead of letting it be, can cause more harm than good.

Everyone is a teacher, everyone is a learner; no matter how self-aware I become, I will still have a course left to learn. As long as I continue to know my own need for learning, I will continue to be humbled to the truth that my greatest teachers will come in various forms—some in forms I never could have imagined.

Being Blind to Love

L ove is an amazing force. It's not just something
that shows up in intimate relationships; it is experienced everywhere people connect. A friend was
once sharing with me her experience with her supervisor.
She worked long hours, often staying well past her scheduled time to complete tasks. Once when her son was sick,
she called into work. Upon her return, her supervisor asked
her to log her hours that she was out. She began to question her supervisor, sharing about the long hours she put in
without overtime pay and asking her boss to see the spirit
of reciprocity she was trying to invoke. The supervisor's
response was simple, "Our place of employment does not
do comp time; sorry." With that, the conversation was over.
She left frustrated and disgruntled.

I told her the issue was not about her; the supervisor simply had an inability to see love when it presented itself.
You see, her long hours at work were not for her personal

benefit; they were a way for her to show love to her supervisor. I shared that if he continued to have blinders to love, eventually her love tank would run dry, and he would be left with an employee who "clocked in" and "clocked out," never willing to give more than minimally expected in her responsibilities.

So often in life, we are blindfolded to love's presence. Love may make itself known in a kind note, a small act of service, a token of appreciation, or through a caring word. If we are not able to see love, then inevitably, we will be unable to see the true direction in which we are to communicate and engage with others. Often before I have a tough conversation with someone, I take a moment and reflect on all the ways the person has shown me love. I then use that reflection to determine whether I need to proceed or the point is moot. Regardless of whether it is in the workplace or at home, take the blindfold off of love, so you can fully see joy, peace, and fulfillment.

Emotionally Disabled

I was having dinner with a friend one day when I received some disturbing news. A mutual friend of ours had been speaking about me in less than flattering ways. I was hurt, saddened, and confused by how this friend had treated me well in one-on-one settings, then spoke of me in a totally different fashion in the company of others. This friend and I had known each other for years, so I understood about his pattern of ineffective behavior in the past. Typically, my nature is to address an issue, to call up someone, share what I had heard said about me, and then work to resolve the conflict. This time was different. I asked myself how I could go about responding with compassion, understanding, and acceptance toward my friend. I thought how it was easy for me to respond with compassion to those with physical and intellectual disabilities, so why shouldn't I employ that same level of ease and compassion with those I know to be emotionally limited in their ability to receive feedback and put it into effective practice?

In the case of my friend, I knew that by giving feedback, all I would do was stunt his future emotional growth. I realized that like a person with intellectual or physical disabilities, until my friend got the proper support, through counseling or other means, to address his needs and past hurts, all my feedback would do would be to exacerbate the emotional scars he was already dealing with.

I am not one to advocate keeping your feelings in or not sharing constructive feedback to support another's journey, but I believe we have to assess the values, patterns, and behaviors of an individual and make an honest assessment of his or her capacity to handle the truth of the situation before we share.

Understanding one's emotional limits is not playing someone small or lowering expectations; it is part of celebrating one of life's great gifts called acceptance: meeting people where they are. When people have not dealt with the emotional wounds that limit their ability to show up effectively, then we who love them are invited to be an inspiration for their potential. We are asked to pray that the needed resources, people, and experiences come to support them, to offer them the lessons that any feedback from us would be limited in providing.

Resentment

I battled with resentment for years. I thought about how to get rid of it until one day, in conversation with my mom, I understood what resentment really is. That day, my mom called me because she was distraught over the way my younger sister was behaving. My mom had recently had an accident at home that had caused her to go to the emergency room. When she returned home, she asked my sister to help her out around the house. My sister did the tasks half-heartedly, and when my mom pointed this out, my sister snapped at her.

Incidences of back and forth bickering between my mother and sister were nothing new. Their relationship was the epitome of hot and cold: some days they were loving toward one other; other days they were in great spaces of hate. When my mom called soon after her accident, I realized something I had never understood before: they resented each other. Their resentment was based in their inability, unwillingness, and downright stubbornness to admit that despite the other's ineffective behaviors, they had deep, deep love for one another.

My sister would get frustrated with my mother because she believed she could never do enough to garner my mother's approval. My mother would get frustrated with my sister because my sister was unable to show care, demonstrate patience, and offer respect toward her. Through it all, the truth never left that they deeply loved one another.

I loved having this conversation with my mom; it offered me a moment of pure self-reflection. I realized the ones I love most, who cause me the most grief, are the same ones I harbor the greatest resentment toward. It was my inability to accept the truth that caused me so much discomfort.

We are asked to make peace with the love we have for other people, understanding their ineffectiveness is a testament to their pain. We must acknowledge that love is a calling beyond our control, and we must accept that the love will not go away, despite our irritation, or the other person's inability to behave how we wish; by reconciling those facts, we begin the process of alleviating resentment and restoring peace.

An Oscar-Winning Performance

When I was in graduate school, a professor of mine said we are always trying to match our insides with other people's outsides. I loved that idea and have found it true in my own life.

I was once at a wedding where I was struck by the father of the bride's demeanor; he had been an absent parent for most of his child's life, and the wedding was the first time he had seen his daughter in a number of years. I expected him to come to the event nervous, pensive, or perhaps slightly ashamed because he was being faced with the reality of all he had missed out on over the course of her young adult life.

To my surprise, his demeanor was just the opposite; he posed confidently in pictures, was sure to let people know the bride was "his daughter," and gave a performance that painted him as the doting dad delivering his daughter to her husband after a lifetime of lavishing care and affection upon her. I was taken aback by his behavior—and put off.

Only years later did I realize what had really happened at the wedding. The truth was the father was not ready to face the truth of what had occurred over the years—the mistakes he had made and the pain others had experienced because of his decisions was too much for him to bear. Rather than explore the pain, have crucial conversations to mend the relationship, and complete those things incomplete, he decided to do what many of us do: avoid.

Avoidance is like taking a Flintstones vitamin for cancer. Avoidance eats you up inside, and eventually, it comes home to roost. For those who experience people with avoidance as a character trait, rather than judge them (as I did at the wedding), find love and compassion for them. Acknowledge that the performance they give must be taxing at times; if you are a person of faith, pray. In any case, take stock of your own life; abide in a space of gratitude that your life has true joy, authentic connections, and real love. In that space, we can see, through all the pain, that it is better to experience what it means to be truly happy than to play a "part" in a script depicting a fantasized version of our life.

Our Drug of Choice

I remember once, after being rejected by a love interest, the feeling of pain, low self-worth and low self-acceptance accompanied that time. In that instant, I wanted to rid myself of the pain by any means necessary. I was like a person looking for a drug to soothe all the woes of the moment. The drug of choice I went to was online dating.

I created my online account, worked on my profile, picked the best pictures, and tried to devise the best one-liners to acquire all of the attention I could. I was so excited, almost high off the expectation of the attention I would receive online. Toward the completion of my profile, a still, small voice stirred in me and said, "This is not the space you're supposed to be in." Confused in that moment, but not one to argue with the still, small voice, I deleted the profile and went to bed sensing the lost possibilities that online dating had to offer.

Only in conversation with a friend several days later did I understand what my exhilaration was really about when I was creating the profile. It came from my addiction to using others to prove I was enough, and I was worthy of love.

I realized the lack of authenticity I was projecting by offering a virtual stranger the power I should have been claiming for myself. So often, I look to other people to validate my worth, to let me know I am enough and loveable. When those people do not live up to my expectations, I feel bad about myself and look to fulfill the drug somewhere else.

It's when we begin to obtain the "drug of choice" in our lives, and say, "No" to that next quick fix that we can begin to reclaim our place of worth. Often, I have lost sight of love and become fixated on someone's ability to show me that I am enough. When the power of our worth is reclaimed, we open up space that allows true love to flourish. Then our high is no longer based on the validation another person offers, but in the genuine love the other person holds for us.

The Elixir to Pain

For years, I held onto pain, not knowing how to rid myself of the constant grief I experienced. Pain gave me security; it gave me the false sense of security that if I am prepared for the worst, nothing can ever get me. It's like being a kid in the kiddie pool; she gets the payoff of knowing her feet are securely fastened to the bottom so she cannot be put in harm's way.

Pain was my lifeline. I would think of those I loved most and how disappointed I would be if they let me down. Those thoughts spontaneously caused large amounts of pain to surface and cloud my joy. In short, pain was a resource I used as a protector when I did not want to activate my faith.

The elixir to pain is 100 percent faith—it's the type of faith that cannot be rattled, that stands through all distractions. It was the type of faith I was being asked to have. I was being asked to surrender to love, to surrender to trusting others. Surrendering to faith was part of my destiny. The call to surrender is challenging to accept and hard to conceive of at times, but nonetheless, it is as real and truthful as any contrived remedy you will come across.

Overdoing It

Nothing feels better than when we understand for ourselves our areas of ineffectiveness. One of the largest areas of ineffectiveness for many I know, including myself, is the blurred line between showing love and being manipulative. Often, particularly in romantic situations, I can go out of my way to be accommodating. I will offer to pick up the person, pay for dinner, or do whatever else I can to be of service. For a long time, I thought this was my way of showing the other person how much I appreciate his time, my excitement about the opportunity to pursue a romantic relationship with him, and a display of just how kind, caring, and loving a person I am.

What was really happening in those moments was an exposure of my own inability to manifest healthy self-worth. What I was doing, rather than showing love, was manipulating the other person into loving me, giving me attention, and showing through his actions his care and consideration for me. Some saw my behaviors as acts of kindness, but others saw them as acts of desperation, and many more saw them as selfish attempts to display kindness with ulterior motives—all of these interpretations were actually true.

While what I am sharing may seem harsh or self-disparaging, it is far from that; it's an acknowledgment of an area of growth that I can take responsibility for with grace and compassion. You see, it is not about being self-critical. It's like trees in a forest—many have been worn and shaken by years of harsh weather, and you can see some of their imperfections in their trunks, the curves of their branches, and the shapes of their leaves. While the tree may not be flawless, it is still no less beautiful and worth appreciating.

When you see yourself overdoing it, coming at people from a place of manipulation, cloaked in the guise of care, take a moment to step back; allow the situation to unfold organically, and begin the conversation, potentially through the help of counseling, to unwrap the root cause of your low self-worth that causes you to act in these unproductive ways.

The Power of No

For years, I would hear people say, "You need to love yourself." I would ponder the phrase "love yourself" and ask myself, "What the hell does that mean?" After years of ruminating on the concept of self-love, I came to understand how it manifests in many ways, such as: the way we speak to others, the way we speak about ourselves, our ability to forgive, and our ability to say, "No."

I love summer, warm weather, and sunny days at the beach—truly my favorite time of the year. But I spent one beautiful summer in a space of resentment and frustration. The reason: I had planned for a leisure-filled summer of fun, but I experienced instead the most hectic and structured summer I could have ever imagined. Every day, minute-by-minute, was structured with planned activities and things on a never-ending to-do list.

After some time, I realized I had done this to myself. It was not work that had caused such clutter to my schedule; it was not family obligations that kept me from the beach; it was all in my inability to say, "No." I would say "Yes" to weddings, "Yes" to special programs, and "Yes" to assisting others, while at the same time saying, "No" to the most important person in my sphere of influence: myself.

When we can reclaim the power of "No," and the power we sometimes relinquish to others in our "Yes," we can begin the joy-filled journey of self-love and liberation.

Fake It Until You Make It

For many readers, healthy self-worth is a constant battle. I long held an image of myself that was far from accurate. I would see myself as dirt, undesirable physically, and desperate in my pursuit to prove I was worth loving. People would say to me, "Darren, you need to work on your self-worth." I could not figure out how to do that—what did it look like to improve your self-worth? Often in conversation, when I am providing my own insights and perspective to others, I gain the greatest nuggets. One of my best friends, like me, struggled for years to find a healthy image of himself. An attractive, intelligent, and driven man, he was plagued by the cancer of insecurity and the disability of low self-worth. One day, in a dark moment, my friend called me for support. I told him how I viewed him: as attractive, intelligent, and driven. He refuted many of my statements, so I asked him, "Do you think I am a liar and untrustworthy?" Taken aback by my question, he quickly replied emphatically, "No." I then asked him, "If you don't think I'm a liar and you feel I'm trustworthy, why can't you trust what I say about you as true? Even if you don't believe it yourself, you can trust that I won't steer you wrong." This scenario is similar to how when we hear a recording of our voice, we don't recognize it because it sounds different from what we hear when we speak; in the same sense, sometimes we cannot accurately see who we are.

I told my friend to learn to fake it until he makes it. He responded, like I am sure many of us would, "How in the hell do I do that?" I said, "Picture that you are someone you think is amazing, smart, driven, and attractive.... This person could be someone you know, look up to, or a celebrity. When life presents you with a challenge, or you try to decide how to respond to matters of the heart, picture yourself as that person, think about how he or she would respond, and then plan your response accordingly. It may feel unfamiliar and weird, but coming to the place of accurately seeing ourselves is weird—just like listening to our voice on an answering machine; it sounds foreign, but give it enough time and sooner, rather than later, it will not feel so out place, and we will feel a little more at home.

Taking my own advice, I have adopted the mantra to "Fake it until you make it." Whatever situation I'm facing, I respond the way I think the person with the attributes I want would. By faking it until I make it, I still face many temptations to revert back to old patterns, and it's a constant fight, but through time, I have seen my commitment and faith lead to manifestations of what I desire in my life. Fake it until you make it, and one day, what seemed to be a sham will show itself to be true.

Food and Fitness

My relationships with food and fitness have often been my greatest indicators of how effectively I can love others. Food is a constant in our lives; we eat to survive, and each time I eat, I am engaging in the exercise of being conscious or unconscious of how I am loving myself. My relationship with food is not based in vanity; it's based in my commitment to be the fullest expression of myself. In life, we are fortunate to be offered the opportunity to inspire others. We serve as a beacon of hope that, despite circumstances, we can all persevere. For me, my physical presence has often been an indicator of this truth.

I work out, think about my eating habits, and keep in mind that my physical presence enhances or limits my full potential and expression. When I don't engage in ongoing conscious eating and fitness, I am not showcasing to those closest to me the value of seeing our bodies as our best friends. Our body is our first friend, the one we first have communion with; we are responsible for putting our body before all other people and things. While this may seem selfish, it's the furthest thing from it; it is the practice of modeling the way for others. As we offer love to ourselves through honoring the bodies we are in, we advance our ability and understanding to do the same for others.

Chapter 6

Shame, Guilt, and Establishing Empathy

The Bill Collector

I have found shame and guilt to be almost like the bill collector in the story of love. For those who have never experienced a bill collector, give gratitude to God; for those who have, I hope this metaphor resonates with you.

When we do not show up well for other people, at times, we can go to a place of shame and guilt. We avoid and do all we can to divert ourselves from facing those things that need to be addressed. Similarly, when a bill collector calls, or we have borrowed money from a friend whom we have not paid back, our tendency is to avoid the person; we dodge phone calls, interactions, or other ways of connecting so we don't have to deal with the unpaid debt. Even when we do connect with that friend, we will do all we can to avoid the unpaid debt conversation. We will talk about the most random topics just to ensure the topic doesn't come up and make us face our lack of integrity.

Unlike a bill collector, however, when we are experiencing the unpaid debts of love, we take it personally, asking why the person is avoiding us, or not interacting with us the way he or she once did. Like a person delinquent on his payments, we prefer to stay comfortable than use discomfort as a tool for growth.

If you have been avoiding the bill collector, know that the only way you will find true liberation is to deal with those unpaid debts from the past. We have to clear the accounts of hurt that we have caused another, and take responsibility for our misbehavior in relationships. On the other end, if you have been the bill collector, wondering how you can go about changing the behavior of others, then in order to open the connection and experience more intimate communication, realize that it is not about you. No matter how kind a bill collector on a phone may be, a person deep in debt will still avoid him. Those who are in debt with love (or with money for that matter), must find the love and strength within themselves to clear up their debts in relationships.

A Warm Welcome

One of my favorite quotes is by Christopher Morley: "Truth, like milk, arrives in the dark, but even so, wise dogs don't bark. Only mongrels make it hard for the milkman to come up to the yard." I love this quote because it speaks to the essence of offering a warm welcome for truth to arrive. I was once running late for an important work event. Stressed and stuck in traffic, I began to feel all sorts of emotions, ranging from anger to fear and frustration. I arrived twenty minutes late for the meeting, feeling full of shame and guilt. I sat quietly, reflecting on my intention to be on time (actually, early), and how my intentions had been thwarted by bad weather and terrible traffic.

When I entered the room, the meeting had already started and members of the team were giving their reports. I was dedicated to my job and the team I supported, so showing up late was beyond hard for me to handle. A couple of minutes after I arrived, our team leader whispered in my ear, "Don't worry about it; we were all running late; the traffic was terrible." In that small moment of grace, the shame I had been holding onto was lifted. What our team leader had provided me with in that small moment was a warm welcome.

In life, many seemingly small moments are really huge nuggets to teach us empathy. I am one to harbor a grudge, slow to forgive, and quick to remind people of when they are wrong. On a much larger scale, I have experienced some of those closest to me arrive metaphorically late for the important events of my life. That metaphorical lateness may be in the form of others being less than truthful, speaking about me in less than loving ways, or being downright unkind. Like me, many people do not intentionally seek to wrong others, but their own traffic jams and weather patterns, called pain and low self-worth, continue to cause them to show up late for life.

Like my team leader, we are all invited, despite people's faults, to give others a warm welcome. That welcome does not make their behavior permissible, but it acknowledges that the ineffectiveness we are experiencing is not about us, but about their inability to manage the traffic and weather in their lives. After my team leader gave me grace, I perked up, shared, and reached out to help in any way I was able. You see, what she provided was grace, what she refrained from was shaming me any more than I was already shaming myself. In her warm welcome and kindness, she gave me permission to allow my true feelings of dedication to come forward. Like my team leader, and like the milkman, when we find strength not to bark (command, demand, and attack), we open space for the truth to shine.

Simulation

I truly believe that everything in life is a simulation for something bigger. To illustrate this point, I will share two stories.

I once was driving when my gas pedal got stuck. I lost control of my car and hit my neighbor's mailbox. I was so overcome with fear, shame, and guilt when I realized the damage I had done to my neighbor's property. While it was through no conscious fault of my own, and the mailbox could be replaced, my guilt was all-consuming. After I found out from my insurance agent how to pay to replace the mailbox, it took me two days to muster up the courage to go to my neighbors with the information. Now, my neighbors were wonderful, incredibly kind people, so I had no reason to fear retaliation from them, but my own internalized shame and guilt paralyzed me from taking action.

Now for a similar story. When I moved to Chicago, one of the first things I did was rent a parking space near my home. Parking in the city can be hard, so a rented space brought me much needed peace of mind. However, each month, without fail, I would be late paying my parking fee. Life would happen, and I would lose track of time and totally forget to pay for my parking. Each month, the owner of my parking space greeted me with kindness, understanding my absentmindedness, and always coming from a place of care. Still, I would become consumed with fear when it would be the middle of the month and I was just then getting around to paying my parking fee. The shame and guilt of not keeping my word at times would get the best of me.

You may look at these two stories and think they were not that significant, but for me, their significance was in the deeper meaning behind them.

These stories served as a simulation for me in my own understanding of shame and guilt. At times, I have experienced people who go for long periods of time without speaking to me. I would wonder, "What did I do? Why is this person avoiding me? Was I not nice enough? Did I say something to offend him/her?" I would, in those moments, make another person's actions all about me.

What the mailbox and the parking space did for me was show

me the power of shame and guilt. If I could be overcome with fear rooted in shame and guilt about a mailbox and a parking space, imagine what that would be like for someone who is truly ineffective in significant areas of his or her life. Think of parents who neglect their children or do not provide for them in ways society expects from parents. Think of a lover or a friend, who shows a lack of integrity and engages in behavior that is destructive to the relationship. If I could feel fear based in shame and guilt about something as small as a mailbox, I can only imagine how fear can manifest in areas of great significance.

Now, I appreciate the mailbox and the parking fee so much more than I ever could have in the moment. They, like many experiences, serve as simulations for larger nuggets of learning; they situate me in a place of empathy, and they allow me to recognize the interconnectedness of the human experience.

Playtime Is Over

E mpathy can be a hard thing to grasp, but whenever we can grasp it in one area, we are giving ourselves clear indication that one day down the road, we will be able to grasp it in another—this is especially true in relation to poor behavior.

I once heard a person say that all money does is exaggerate the qualities a person already possesses. Meaning, if you were a difficult and stubborn person before you had money, you will be even more so with it. The same goes for ineffective behavior in adults, but rather than money being the exaggerator of those qualities, it is maturation. For example, if you were courageous and independent as a child, you will most likely possess those same qualities as an adult. If you were limited in your self-expression as a child, you will be limited in your self-expression as an adult.

This rule of maturation can be so critical for understanding empathy because in many instances, we say things like, "Why are you doing this?" or "Why are they doing that?" or the even more common phrase, "Why don't you act your age?" The truth is that the person is acting her age; she is acting as the exaggerated version of her younger self. If she had a hard time managing anger at age seven, then when you experience her at age twenty-seven mismanaging her emotions, rather than say, "Act your age" or "Grow up," realize she is just showing up as the exaggerated seven-year-old version of herself.

For those of us who still find this situation frustrating, it might be helpful for us to look at when our own youthful acts were ineffective for us, remember how they had a negative impact on others, and think about how we might still be experiencing those same ineffective behaviors in our adult lives. We all have to face that mighty and hard truth that we are not kids anymore. At some point, the childish ways of our past will cause us difficulty, disappointment, and regret if we don't recognize that playtime is over, and the time is now to make the transformation into the powerful and beautiful person we were destined to be.

Chapter 7
Repeating the Cycle

We Have Something in Common

Often, I find myself being tempted to judge others and asking myself questions such as, "How can he do that?" or "What was she thinking?" However, this judgmental behavior changed for me one fateful day in September.

At the time, I found myself frustrated with a relationship where the other person seemed always to be withholding—he was open to hearing my perspective but limited in his willingness to share anything of himself. To say I was frustrated was an understatement. But my frustration changed to empathy when my friends confronted me about how I withhold and don't fully share myself with others. Basically, I was engaging in the same behavior that had caused me frustration.

I realized that in an environment where the majority of people were white and straight, I would feel out of place as a black gay man; feeling internalized self-hate, I would not express myself fully. I was afraid of how others would respond to me. Would they reject me? Would they cast me from the group, or make me feel even more out of place than I already felt?

In a split second, I was stopped in my tracks. I could see empathy, feel empathy, and taste the peace that comes from understanding someone else's experiences. Too often, I would climb to the mountaintop of self-righteousness, not even realizing I was visiting it, and at times, I would even set up long-term residency in the valley of hypocrisy.

One of my favorite things in the world is to talk with dear friends and family about their hopes, fears, and disappointments. I often thought my keen ability to listen to friends share their struggles was my inner counselor coming out. Now I know that those closest to me have become a mirror of sorts—because I am gaining in my awareness that we are not all that different. We are all invited to consider how insecurity and doubt manifest in all of us at times. To that end, it's our ability to see those moments of insecurity within ourselves and others that puts us on the path to bringing about our heart's greatest desires.

Karma

S o much of love stems from the relationship we first form with our parents. When I began dating, I found many of my parents' traits showing up as characteristics in those with whom I considered having relationships.

One time, a friend was sharing with me her concerns and struggle with a partner who was non-communicative. I asked my friend whether she had ever been in a situation where she had shown up that way. Surprised by the question, her response was an emphatic "No." I asked about her father, since she had previously mentioned having a strained relationship with him. She had said that, at times, she had been non-communicative with her dad—the same way her partner was behaving toward her.

I suggested that perhaps she should tend to the relationship with her father by being more open; perhaps in doing so, she would learn a few things. When my friend mentioned how difficult it would be, I said, "Good. Perhaps then you will have greater empathy for what your partner struggles with in being in a relationship with you."

One of the great blessings of life is when we realize we have treated others poorly in similar ways to how we are currently being treated. When we see how we have been the prognosticators of indifference in a relationship, we are then empowered to transform that indifference into a relationship full of adoration, fidelity, and love.

Denver

O ne of my favorite movies is the film adaptation of Toni Morrison's book *Beloved.* The movie is set during the days right after slavery. In the film, a mother named Sethe, who has experienced years of shame, guilt, and unworthiness, based on her decision to kill her young child, Beloved, rather than see her child grow up in the horror of slavery, finds herself in a place of perceived redemption and acceptance when her daughter miraculously comes back from the dead, years later, in human, adult form.

From the time of Beloved's death, to her return, Sethe has other children, including a daughter named Denver. Denver loves her mother and devotes her life to supporting her; even when the other children leave home, Denver stays. When Beloved returns, she brings turmoil and chaos to the home. Beloved's actions rob Denver of joy, peace, and the experience of fully feeling love. Sethe, so happy to see Beloved's return, becomes blind to all the ways that Beloved is causing harm and turmoil to the family. In addition, she puts all her time, care, and attention into trying to please Beloved, with total disregard for Denver. Through it all, Denver is left to fend for herself, all the while still remaining steadfast in her dedication to her mother.

I love the film so much because I can relate to it. When I was eleven, my mother suggested I go live with my father. Up to that point, my relationship with my father had been strained. Only seeing each other once a year in the summer, neither one of us knew the other very well. In addition, my father had proven himself to be someone unable to fulfill his promises, someone who did not contribute well (financially or emotionally) to my support, and someone who would say hurtful things to me.

When I moved in with my father, I was so eager to earn his acceptance and love that I did everything I could to gain his approval. While he would say hurtful things about my weight or my effeminate disposition, none of that mattered to me; I just wanted his acceptance. The energy I put into gaining my father's acceptance came at the expense of my relationship with my mother. My mother, from the time of my birth until I left to live with my father, had been my emotional and financial supporter; with the support of my maternal grandmother, she had been my everything. But when I went to live with my father, I totally divested all energy from my relationship with my mother and grandmother. I never called home to see how my mom was doing; it was like I was now with my father, and I needed to give all care, time, and attention to him. My father had become the "idol" that I had made into the holder of my worth. Not until years later, when I was being disregarded by another, did I realize the pattern I had created for myself.

Like Sethe and me, many of us go through stages when our self-acceptance is low and shame has taken hold of our lives; we then place power in others' hands to change our own self-perceptions. In Sethe's case, Beloved became that placeholder, and for me, it was my dad. Like Sethe, though, what I was oblivious to was how my own low self-worth was causing others pain. Denver and my mother, who both in their respective relationships had given nothing but love and dedication, became the bearers of another person's alienation, and the victims of another person's pain and low self-worth.

Many of us dedicate ourselves to others, so we are at a loss when those people seem to disregard our love and consideration. We see these people shower others with love and affection at the expense of showing care and attention to us. We ask questions like, "How could you do this to me?" and "Can't you see how much I love you?" We see ourselves metaphorically being like Denver. However, we can take solace in knowing it is often not a lack of love that keeps people from showing love and dedication; it is their inability to harness within themselves the power to be their own manufacturers of self-worth and acceptance. When we look to others to provide us with the worth we should be cultivating from within, we become like Sethe, incubators of pain and alienators of the ones who demonstrate love to us the most.

Chapter 8

Our Greatness

This Little Light of Mine

In her book *A Return to Love*, Marianne Williamson speaks about our greatest fear by saying:

> Our deepest fear is not that we are inadequate. Our deepest fear is that we are powerful beyond measure. It is our light, not our darkness that most frightens us. We ask ourselves, Who am I to be brilliant, gorgeous, talented, fabulous? Actually, who are you *not* to be? You are a child of God. Your playing small does not serve the world. There is nothing enlightened about shrinking so that other people won't feel insecure around you. We are all meant to shine, as children do. We were born to make manifest the glory of God that is within us. It's not just in some of us; it's in everyone. And as we let our own light shine, we unconsciously give other people permission to do the same. As we are liberated from our own fear, our presence automatically liberates others.

So often, I have seen how true it is that our greatness scares us. We often listen to our inner voices of why we are not good enough, what we need to do differently, etc., instead of acknowledging the lie we are telling ourselves.

I remember having a conversation with a friend—a bright, beautiful, intelligent woman—who had just applied to get her Ph.D. Knowing that, you would think she would be the epitome of confidence, but to the contrary. Like many of us, when met with relationships that were not working as well as she had anticipated, she began the questioning process: "What is wrong with me? Am I worthy of being loved?" The voice in our head that talks to our insecurities is the same one that often wants to deplete us of joy. I reminded my friend that I knew her as smart, beautiful, and caring. I gave her facts, rather than the fictitious stories that came from her ego, which was addicted to inflicting pain. By the time I was done sharing all the facts—where she went to college, how she was applying to Ph.D. programs, and her host of accomplishments—she began to laugh. See, that is the true beauty of it—when we are faced with the facts of who we are for others, we often find humor in the fallacy that we are not enough.

Another friend of mine dreamt of going to law school and pursuing a career as a non-profit law specialist. Her goal was set and her determination was steadfast. She applied to one school, and one school only: her dream school. While her LSAT scores were low, she had hope that she would get into graduate school. Once she was offered admittance, she was elated, overjoyed that her dream could come true. But as the time drew near for her to go to school, she became fearful, asking questions about what it would be like to move, and how much debt would be incurred in the process. These were all valid questions, but it was evident that her questioning was based on her own fears. The fears were not in the questioning, but in the realization that she could soon have her dreams manifest into reality. Often, we, as humans, embrace and foster comfort rather than lean into the fear of the unknown—at the risk of coming alive. We invite the opportunity to play small because, as Williamson so eloquently puts it, it is our light, not our darkness, that most frightens us.

Don't Dim Your Light

U ntil well into my twenties, I would find friends who would serve as pace setters for me. These friends would be the ones I would look up to, be inspired by, and go to in times when I needed personal or professional coaching. I have always had an inner drive to succeed, but often that drive was muted by others' achievements, meaning that if I thought you could run a mile in ten minutes, well, I would pray I could do it in eleven. I never thought I could run faster, perform higher, or shine brighter than those around me. I just did not think it was possible.

A series of unfortunate events changed all of this for me. As with many relationships, I saw those same pace setters that had marked much of my career begin to move in different directions—our values began to shift, and I became lost, not knowing what to do without the support of my pace setters around me. All this was exacerbated by the fact that I began to experience what it felt like for others to be jealous of my success. I began to feel guilty and was tempted to dim my light so I could maintain my community. I would refrain from sharing my successes and hopes. At the time, I would have argued that I was practicing humility like any good person should, but in actuality, fear of my own light was keeping me from sharing.

Writing this book has been one of the greatest exercises I have ever participated in to break my habit of dimming my own light. Each of us has a calling, and that calling can come in many forms and offer great benefits by following it. What I have come to understand is that another person's inability to master the wattage of his or her own light does not give me the permission to mismanage mine. In a space of faith, I have come to a place of peace; I realize that the same God, who is committed to me living the fullest expression of my life, is committed to those around me doing the same.

One thing I know for sure is that the journey to let yourself be fully expressed, and the opportunity to manifest your greatest potential, can be lonely. In a world riddled with fear and insecurity, people can only celebrate others up to the point that they can celebrate themselves. What we all can do is love people enough to liberate ourselves from depending on them to reinforce our light, and liberate them to make the decision for themselves of how bright their contributions on earth will be.

FLOTUS

Regardless of your political affiliation, it is hard to dispute the ways Michelle and Barack Obama have offered proof to the truth of the American Dream. As two African-American individuals who came from their own sets of difficult circumstances, they have ascended to the highest points in American politics and influence. I have especially come to enjoy watching how Michelle Obama has been able inspire millions around the world.

Once, I was working with a group that was looking for a speaker for an event. I told them to shoot for the stars and suggested the President. Their response, half-jokingly, was, "Why would we want President Obama when we can have Michelle?" I laughed and conceded that the First Lady of the United States (FLOTUS), Michelle Obama, would be an equally notable choice as a speaker.

From the outside, what I see as striking about the First

Lady is her ability to hold her own space and make a name for herself separate from anyone else. Certainly, she is a mother, a wife, a daughter, a sister, and a friend, but beyond all of the titles associated with her, she is Michelle. She is a woman who, in her own right, has utilized her values to strive to be the fullest expression of herself. Mrs. Obama can be seen with dignitaries speaking about international affairs, and moments later, playing with inner-city kids on the White House lawn.

I remember watching CNN one morning when the pundits began speculating whether Mrs. Obama herself would one day run for political office. While I disregarded much of what they said as political fodder, I did have to acknowledge the great compliment being paid to her in their observation that she could be a political force.

What sticks out for me about the First Lady is that during her time in the White House, she always has maintained her commitment to move beyond limitations and achieve her full potential.

In each relationship we enter, we are afforded the same opportunity to be our own version of FLOTUS. Perhaps we may not get to dine with dignitaries or influence government policy. Rather, perhaps our dining is in a classroom of students as a teacher, our influence is in our local neighborhood, or in a clinic as a healthcare provider. Wherever your truth and potential lie, do all you can to maximize it.

I have seen friends ask where love is as they battle substance abuse. Others ask where love is as they seek the courage and means to discern a vocational path. Many others ask where love is as they continue to use food as a comfort to pain. Asking where love is, when we are not moving in the direction of our full potential and truth, is like trying to strike up conversation with the dead: pointless.

I don't know the First Lady personally, but I would assume that she has known disappointment like any of us, and she has faced hardship and loss like we all have. What she has also done, that many of us struggle at doing, is harness her power and inner resilience to allow her potential to be fully expressed when the temptation to do otherwise is imminent.

Get Behind the Wheel

I have seen people talk themselves out of jobs, schooling opportunities, and decisions that would dramatically alter their lives in the most positive of ways.

For a long time, I wondered why people would engage in behavior that would block them from experiencing the greatest expression of themselves. What I am now learning and trying to master is the understanding that sometimes people engage in these behaviors because they find it more comfortable to be mediocre than to go out on a limb and be great.

For those who struggle with this concept, picture being sixteen and learning to drive. You bought your cousin's old 1985 Honda Civic, and you are feeling pretty comfortable, so you give it some gas and you accidently bump into a pole. But at this point, who cares? The car has over 200,000 miles on it, and rust along the side shows it has known better days, so you give yourself subconscious permission to be a little more carefree. Now, if we take that 1985 Honda Civic and make it a brand new Mercedes, the experience changes slightly. The carefree experience of driving now becomes this tiring experience of stress. You now watch every turn and are super-cautious, afraid that one wrong move could dent the bumper or scratch the car. Fear overcomes you to the point that in some ways you miss the old Honda. You think to yourself, "At least in the old Honda, I had peace, less responsibility, and fewer worries."

This analogy holds true in other areas of our lives, and in the lives of the ones we love the most. For some of us, to realize our greatest potential in vocational and romantic pursuits is like driving the brand new car—we get nervous and afraid of the pain; if we fail in the pursuit, the devastation will be too much to bear. We get into mediocre relationships, compromise our standards, and develop intimate partnerships with people who do not meet the match of our potential. We settle, rather, for the used Honda, feeling secure in knowing if we dent it, it will not cause major damage. In relationships, we settle, resting on the laurels of a partner who does not meet our match for a mate, but provides security. Or worse, we settle on a mate, fearing that no one else will want us, so this is the best we can do. As we move through life, we are continually invited to consider which wheel we are going to drive behind. Do we play our lives small and go behind the wheel of what is safe, or do we dare greatly by pursuing our full potential and worth with faith in our own ability? What I am continually reminded of is that I falter in fear and find favor in faith.

High Class Dining

When we ask others about their hopes, aspirations, and dreams, rarely do they respond, "I want ordinary love, an ordinary job, an ordinary income, and an ordinary life." While that may not be what we say, it is certainly how we act.

I was on the phone with a friend who was supervising a man with a promising career ahead of him. He had just finished graduate school—the first in his family to go to college, a shining beacon of hope after coming from an upbringing filled with challenges. Soon after getting into his position, however, he began to display dysfunctional behaviors in the workplace. My friend called me, seeking counsel on how to support her staff member. She said, "I don't understand; it's like he is engaging in self-sabotaging behaviors." At that moment, I comprehended just how often, when we are on the brink of the biggest breakthroughs of our life and blessings of great abundance are in our midst, we engage in self-sabotaging behavior.

I was confused and could not understand why we, as humans, do not embrace everything that is good and great to us until I compared the situation to high class dining. My first time going to an expensive restaurant, I was insecure because I didn't know which fork to use or how to pronounce everything on the menu—I was out of my comfort zone. Others around me were surprised by my demeanor and taken aback by my lack of excitement to be at this restaurant. After the meal was over (which I had mainly picked over), I went straight to a popular fast-food restaurant. I knew just what to order; I knew exactly what it would taste like, and I was back in my comfort zone. Rather than speak to my insecurities at the expensive restaurant, ask for support through the experience, or even try to situate myself in a place of possibly fitting into this new environment, I just settled for the idea that as soon as the meal was over, I would head straight for the cheap junk food I was accustomed to.

The prosperity destined for our lives is the same way. When we find love with an amazing person, we turn away in fear and discomfort. When we find ourselves experiencing new opportunities beyond anything we knew growing up, we self-sabotage, secretly (and sometimes unknowingly) yearning for the comfort of the mediocre spaces where we were before.

The next time I see someone engaging in behavior in direct contradiction to the gifts God wants to manifest in his or her life, I will not get angry or become confused. Rather, I will think about my first high class dining experience and the comfort I craved in simple junk food. The lesson for us all: We are blessed in our capacity to receive.

Lions & Lambs

One of the most disheartening things I have ever experienced is the distance that occurs in relationships. So often in the past when my relationships seemed to move in different directions, where interactions lessened and a remaining connection was hard to find, I would become self-critical and do all I could to throw out a life preserver to save the relationship. Over time, what I have come to understand is that on my own pathway to truth, distance may naturally occur with those I hold most dear because our pathways are meant to go in different directions.

Lions do not lie down with lambs. To be clear, I am not defining a lion by worldly measures of success. A lion, for me, is anyone who has the tenacity and self-efficacy to be bold in the pursuit of truth.

When I am behaving like a lion—daring greatly to excel to new heights and to accomplish greater things—I have slowly and painfully had to realize that not everyone will want to join that journey. I would lecture, become judgmental, and downright harass those around me to move in the way I moved. However, what I have come to learn is that when distance occurs, one of two things is happening: either others are being placed in a laboratory to learn, or we are being invited to grow in our own way with the end result of a greater expression and manifestation of ourselves. As we grow into the lion we are destined to be, either others will do the same, or we will not care anymore. In both scenarios, we are left with peace, which should be our ultimate goal.

Now, when distance occurs in a relationship, rather than try to manipulate others to change, I seize the moment to work on my *roar*. To work on my roar means to situate myself in environments that challenge me to live up to my fullest potential—physically, mentally, emotionally, and spiritually. What I know for sure is that manipulation has never led anyone I know to change; rather, change has always transpired through inspiration.

If you are striving to be a lion, surround yourself with a strong pack of lions. If you are looking to get fit, surround yourself with a fit pack of lions. If you are looking to grow in your spiritual journey, surround yourself with a spiritually astute set of lions. If you are looking for financial liberation, surround yourself with lions who are financially free. This may seem like common sense, a practice we have often heard before, but it is no less true. The reason why it can sometimes be dismissed is because of the difficulty and pain of letting go—that is, having the courage and strength to leave your herd of lambs for a new pack of lions. But you must leave—even the greatest of lions will eventually see himself as a lamb if that is all he surrounds himself with.

Water into Wine

When my sister first started dating, she came to me for some brotherly advice. I told her that in life we see ourselves in one of two ways: water or wine. Water is a substance that, for many of us, is easy to come by. We turn on a faucet and fill a plastic cup; if it spills, no worries—it is just water. Wine, however, specifically really nice wine, we put in a long stem glass. We perhaps serve it with a good meal and maybe even dress up for the occasion.

As humans, we can be treated like we are water or wine. Sometimes others can treat us cheaply, putting us in their own version of a plastic cup, drinking us at their leisure. If they spill us (inflict hurt), it's not a problem, because since we're like water to them, it's not that big of a deal.

Conversely, when we are treated like wine, people will do what they can to uplift us (put us in a long stem glass), treat us with care, and rise to the occasion (dress up) to be with us.

When I originally shared this analogy with my sister, I told her she had to discern for herself whether she was water or wine. If she saw herself as wine, she should show up as such and expect others to treat her in kind. What I now know that I did not know then is that not only do we need to see ourselves as wine, but we also have to understand that as with alcohol, there is an age when it is appropriate to drink. Sometimes people treat us like water because they themselves have not matured enough to be metaphorically legally old enough to drink wine. I have found that whether I am treated like water or wine is less about the demand I put on others, and more about my own ability to detect whether someone is metaphorically of legal drinking age and has the spiritual maturity to regard me like wine.

The Truth Shall Set You Free

A couple of years ago, I committed one of the most courageous acts I could have ever imagined—I told every secret I had. That's right; everything I had used as a burden of shame, I shared. I shared it with close friends, and I shared it with my mother—many of those truths I shared I speak to in this book, such as being gay, the abuse inflicted upon me, and the abuse I inflicted upon others. I have come to learn over the years that telling the truth about ourselves is one of the greatest acts of self-love. The truth is our declaration that while our actions may not be popular and may not support our moral and ethical positions, we are still worthy of sharing our truth, and it is up to the receiver of that information how to handle it.

When we are honest with ourselves and those around us, we liberate not only ourselves, but future generations to come. So often, I will hear friends share how they want their children to live free, honest, and open lives. But often, my response is, "How can your children be free, honest, and open when you are not modeling that now in your own life?" When we speak our truth, we practice self-love; when we speak our truth, we abolish shame, fear, and guilt; when we speak our truth, we make the ultimate plea for freedom.

Perseverance

Chapter 9

In the Meantime

The Breakthrough

P erseverance is one of the greatest virtues an individual can possess. Attention is frequently given to
the promise of the future, but little conversation is
had about the lead up to that promise. What I have come to
learn over the years is that every breakdown is a set up for
a breakthrough. In every occasion of my life, I have asked
myself in the midst of life's great disappointments, "What
is the lesson in this moment? What is the higher ground
that I am being asked to reach?" I have learned the great
truth that every breakdown is building our emotional and
spiritual muscle for the breakthrough on the other side. In
discussions with friends and family, I have come to see a
pattern—how their greatest disappointments were preparation for their capacity to handle the promise on the other
side.

My mom has shared with me her personal stories of financial hardship, disappointment, and job loss; she has shared

how those breakdowns opened up space for humility, for patience, and for gratitude. In that space, she found herself years later in a better job, a better home, and with a better overall quality of life. Had she not experienced the breakdown, she never would have been prepared for the breakthrough.

All this may sound familiar, and for some who read these words, it may come off as being ethereal or playing Pollyanna's "Glad Game," but there is nothing fantasy-based about this at all. The only way the breakdown does not manifest into a breakthrough is if we do not couple perseverance with its friend resilience. It's one thing to persist through the situation; it is another to couple it with resilience. For me, resilience is the ability to see the problem, ask what the lesson is, and get about the business of making change happen.

In my biggest breakdowns, I have turned to my faith, a therapist, and personal healthy habits (exercise and eating right) to get me through life's storms. In those moments, I saw my faith as the anchor to guide my path, therapy as a tool to provide me with a clear perspective, and healthy habits as a way to say to God, the Creator, the Universe, or whatever name you give the force greater than yourself, that I am getting myself prepared for the breakthrough.

Practicing resilience during the breakdown is hard; it's so easy to pick up a bag of chips and eat away our pain, curse the notion of God and faith, and say, "To hell with therapy; I can manage this on my own." What I know for sure is that if we are really dedicated to seeing the fullest manifestations of ourselves and the lives we lead come to pass, we must do the work to see every breakdown as the set up to the breakthrough.

Today Is the Tomorrow You Thought You Could Not Face the Day Before

In the movie *Kingdom Come*, one of the main characters, played by Cedric the Entertainer says, "Today is the tomorrow you thought you could not face the day before." When I heard that, I asked my sister, who was watching the movie with me, what she thought the tomorrow that we both would not be able to face would be. Without a second thought, my sister said the passing of our maternal grandmother. I soon agreed that the passing of our maternal grandmother would be that day I certainly would not be able to face. I told my sister that the day my grandmother passed would be the day I would jump off the roof because the pain would be too much for me to handle. Without advance illness, or warning, three days later my grandmother had a sudden heart attack and died. There in that moment, I was faced with the day I thought I could not face the day before. I wish losing my grandmother had been the only time I experienced that truth, but alas, that has not been the case. In my own journey of love, I have found so many occasions when I have thought of hard moments that I have later seen come to pass—moments of rejection, of love not being reciprocated, of being hurt by others—so many moments that, in the past, I would have said would have been too much for me to bear.

Through each situation, I found an inner strength; some call that type of strength resilience. The truth I have derived from each of these experiences is that life has equipped me for more than I thought possible. Through each disappointment and every moment of grief, I discovered that on the other side was a gift. With the passing of my grandmother, the gift was an understanding of the power of sharing gratitude daily. And it was with the disappointment and grief on the journey to see love's promise that I was presented with the gift of the inspiration for this book. Certainly, today can be the tomorrow we thought we could not face the day before, but just as certain is the assurance that abundance is on the other side of that dreaded day if we have the tenacity and patience to endure.

In the Meantime

One of the most difficult things to grasp is the end of a relationship. The heartbreak, sense of loss, and despair that accompany the end of an intimate relationship can disrupt peace like few other things. When we are in pain, we are invited to move with faith, knowing this piece of the narrative is over, but the story of our lives is far from complete.

Too often, we sit and contemplate the "how" of "How will I get through this tough time now that my relationship is over? What am I supposed to do with myself?" Instead, I suggest to people that they look at life from the place of "the meantime." While we are waiting for the former relationship to be made whole, or the new relationship to emerge, we can focus on the meantime. The meantime is the space where we can reflect on what areas of life need our attention—perhaps a relationship with a parent or other loved one needs our attention; perhaps an area of our life or a person needs our forgiveness, or perhaps we need to ask for forgiveness. Perhaps we need to focus on our own self-love; perhaps we have neglected our own physical, financial, spiritual, and emotional health during this relationship. For many others, the meantime is simply a byproduct of the "not yet" (a concept I'll touch on in further detail later in this book).

The not yet may be less about repairing a relationship with others or ourselves, and more about life telling you now is not the time. I have had several friends who have either been in the midst of their careers or the throes of school ask me why they were single. I would tell them the answer is simple—you don't have the time to be otherwise. Sometimes, the meantime is less about what we need to do differently and more about timing. In other words, it's not the right season. It's like living in the Southern United States and wearing a fleece coat in the middle of July; it is the wrong clothing for the wrong season. But just as surely as summer comes after spring, so too will autumn follow summer, and then the season will come when your fleece coat will be appropriate.

Whatever the questions are in your life, begin to inquire about your own season of life and you will see that you can find hope and peace in the meantime until the storm of heartbreak and despair has passed.

Seek Wise Counsel

There are internal and external processors. I, for one, have become quite proficient at processing my thoughts externally. Whatever I am feeling, good or bad, as long as you have an ear to listen, I have a mouth willing to communicate. So it took time for me to learn one critical lesson about when I process with others—to seek wise counsel.

Now, rather than process with everyone, or debate issues in others' company, I first give a personal assessment of the other person's values against my own. It's not an assessment of "good" or "bad"; it's a simple evaluation to understand whether we are in the same lane. Once I was in conversation with a dear friend; we were discussing general topics of the day. As he shared his perspective, I soon realized that we were approaching life from two fundamentally different domains. It is one thing to have separate views, but an entirely different thing to enact practices that reflect divergent values.

At that moment, I took stock of the conversation, what I was learning, and the lesson to be learned therein that my friend would not be one from whom I would seek wise counsel. In life, we have to find out who those wise counselors are; they may be friends, or they may not be. They are those people who live lives that we would want to emulate, or they experience prosperity in the areas we care most about. In short, the wisest counsel is administered by those who are true to themselves. Identify those who serve such a role for you, and those who may not drive in the same lane of life as you. However much love is there, seek wise counsel to ensure you do not lose sight of your own course and you stay true to it.

Chapter 10

Pain

Grieving the Possibility

On either side, the end of a relationship can be hard to grapple with. Whether you are the person who ended the relationship, or the person who is experiencing another's desire to discontinue a relationship, both positions can be hard. I have sat in great sorrow at seeing loss occur. I have sat in the place of wonder, thinking about what could have been. What I was failing to realize is I was sitting in the land of "could," and not what was. I was grieving the possibility and not what the situation was in reality.

In reality, I was experiencing a relationship that was less than fulfilling, and while the possibility was great, the actual relationship was challenging to manage when the other person was often emotionally unavailable.

On the other side, I have had friends who have terminated relationships and then looked back, grieving in the land of possibility. At times, I have offered them a reminder that when they were with their former lover, they complained, felt like they were being smothered, and moved in a place of fear where they engaged in avoidance relationship patterns. Now, they are left with the decision they made and are being asked to make peace with it.

Reconciling grief over possibility and living with reality is hard. Accepting things as they were does not mean we must relinquish faith in the future. To accept is simply to acknowledge that the relationship came to an end for a reason and that joy's fullest expression could not have occurred in it.

Color Blind

Often in life, we find ourselves in spaces where we experience pain—pain so severe that it can be almost debilitating. I had a friend who was going through a hard time in a relationship; the relationship had hit an impasse and a flood of emotions swept her way. Feelings of low self-worth, of not being loved, and of a partner who did not reciprocate the love she held for him put her in a space of fear and insecurity.

After I let her share the things she had "conjured" as proof of her feelings, I shared with her counter-facts to the facts she had constructed; they were not opinions, just facts. In this case, she had a partner who contributed to her financially, who in difficult times had lent his support not only to her, but also to her extended family. I offered to her that every time he showed love to her extended family, he was in essence showing love to her. I asked her why a man who had no care for her would financially contribute to her life without any inherent responsibility to do so. I asked her why he would stay with her all these years if he did not love her.

After my barrage of questions, she began to laugh because she realized "the proof" she had taken as evidence that their love was not real, was, in fact, false. I invited her to understand that she experienced the relationship from an inaccurate viewpoint, that in my questioning, all I had done was provide a space for her to see a counterargument to what she had created.

I asked her to consider how she could go about healing that inaccurate view. I suggested to her, "It's like being color blind; you see browns as burgundy. You see the UPS truck and you say, 'Wow, that truck is a rich shade of burgundy.' Your friend counters, 'No, that is not burgundy; it's brown.' You continue back and forth until your friend retorts, 'If it were burgundy, why would its tagline be, "What can brown do for you?"' At this point, you laugh at the acknowledgment that your sight is not accurate and there may be something that needs to be attended to."

Similarly, when people reveal that love is present in our lives, we are quick to argue that it is not there. If we sit still and allow truth to present itself, more often than not, we will see that we are just wearing blinders to love's presence. When we realize that our sight is incorrect, we can begin the real work of healing—perhaps that is through forgiveness (a central tenet of this book), in counseling, or sorting through old pains. Whatever the case may be, do not allow your blindness to persist so long that you lose full sight of the love another is trying to offer you.

The Fallacy of Pain

For the longest time, I thought pain was something real, but over time, I have seen that pain is just a force the ego uses to displace us from the road of truth. When I look back over my life at all of the things that have brought me the greatest pain, I see that each one has turned out to be a temporary roadblock in my journey to truth. What an amazing feat for all of us if we could believe that pain was not real, and that peace was the only thing rooted in truth. If we believe in the fallacy of pain, then what we are experiencing in the now is the not yet on the pathway to our destiny. To quote Esther Hicks, "Everything you are going through is preparing you for what you asked for."

Once, I was on vacation with family, and an unrequited love was in the same town where we were vacationing. While I was there, I got word that this person had entered into a new relationship; immediately, I was overcome with pain and I wanted to shut down because of the past rejection. In that moment, I remembered the lesson from *A Course in Miracles* that pain is not real. I thought to myself, "If for an instant, I claimed that my feelings were untrue and what I was experiencing was not real, how would I then react?"

Later that day, I took stock of where I was, realizing the relationship I dreamed of was not one I actually had time for. You see, I was in my final year of a Ph.D. program with exams and a dissertation to write; all I had time for was school. And this pain was just my ego's strategy to knock me off my course.

Stay the course; remind yourself that pain is not real and peace is always the home of truth. So often, we give unfair power to our feelings. For example, if someone does something that hurts us, automatically we go to the freezer for ice cream to give us comfort, or to the couch to curl up in a blanket for relief, or toward the ear of a loved one to share our discomfort. In those moments, we give all our power to the feelings and perpetuate the myth that our feelings control our actions. The truth is that you and only you control your actions.

Once in a conversation with my mom, I told her that I love the gym and regard it as a spiritual experience for me. No matter how bad my feelings, no matter how hurt or sad, happy or mad I am, I always go to the gym. Some days, the pain can feel so real that all I can do is muster the strength to walk ten minutes on the treadmill. In those moments, it's not about the experience of working out, or how much weight I lift, or how far/fast I run; it's about me making the declaration that I have control of my life, that feelings do not power my action, and that pain is a fallacy.

Jealousy Is Pain's Attempt to Project Outwardly

When someone does something negative to us, we tend to ask ourselves, "What did I do wrong?" and "What could I have done differently?" Years ago, I read Don Miguel Ruiz's *The Four Agreements*. Ruiz says that to take things personally is breaking one of those most coveted agreements, but it was only recently that I saw the truth in that statement.

I was talking to a friend, who was having a difficult time in his job and feeling unhappy and unfulfilled. I could tell he was frustrated by his seemingly never-ending dissatisfaction with his work. Later that evening, my friend called another mutual friend of ours; this other person was in a very different place. Motivated and feeling purpose in his work, he often showed up happy, carefree, and full of promise. The dialogue between the two friends was less than healthy, with the unhappy friend taunting the other with information he knew would be hurtful. After the conversation, my happy, carefree friend was crying, confused, and not knowing what to make of what had happened in the exchange. What was taking place was an interaction based in jealousy. My friends' interaction wasn't the first time I had experienced jealousy.

I had a close friend who for many years served as an inspiration to me. As I continued to find success on my path, while he was met with difficulties on his, the friendship took a turn, and the relationship that started in love, became a harbor of resentment. My friend became distant, finding opportunities to speak of me negatively via social media and other outlets. Hurt, I confronted my friend, offering him space to share his disdain, with my earnest attempt to mend the relationship. In the conversation, I realized he was in pain; his pain was causing him to act out, displacing responsibility for his unhappiness onto me. What I had been experiencing was not an impasse in a relationship but the infiltration of jealousy. In its simplest terms, jealousy is nothing more than another person's inaccurate perception of someone else's journey. My friend thought I had it easy, when in reality, I was experiencing some of the most difficult seasons of my life: facing old childhood hurts, being confronted with the need to forgive, managing my own life and a host of responsibilities…at the time, spending consistent time in therapy to learn how to respond effectively to current and past emotional wounds. My friend's inaccurate depiction of my life was based on false assumptions because he did not have the courage, or perhaps care enough, to ask me about my journey.

Jealousy is a manifestation of fear, and fear is a bastardization of love. In those moments, I saw jealousy, I saw how it is employed and how it truly is pain's attempt to project outwardly. What I know for sure is that if jealousy is not transformed into inspiration, it will cause a person's self-destruction.

Gas on E

Throughout my life, I have often thought that if only this person did this, or if only that person did that, then the situation would be okay. What I have realized, though, is the power of manipulating others to help temporarily mask pain. For me, the pain was insecurity, which stemmed from the stories I told myself of not being enough and of my inability to give and receive love. The stories were the product of my having an absent parent, which led to anxiety and caused me to commit one of those ungrateful acts in the practice of love: smothering.

Smothering is a disease brought about by anxiety. I noticed that I would be self-disciplined and self-aware enough not to smother until the relationship was invited to the next level. As soon as I felt someone was offering to deepen his commitment to me, I would become afraid and filled with anxiety. I would become addicted to constant communication, using it as my drug of choice to keep me in a constant state of security. It was only after much disappointment that I realized I really did not want to be in constant communication with the other individual; instead, I was using him as a temporary fix to deal with my anxiety. Rather than share with him that I was insecure and experienced anxiety when we didn't speak, I would find passive means to communicate: continuous texts, over-sharing via email, or other forms of written communication to try to dominate and control his engagement in our relationship.

What I have come to realize is that smothering is the antithesis of love; it is an act of using another person to fill the void of your own pain. Individuals are meant to share the journey with us, not *do* the journey for us. To illustrate this point, imagine you're driving your car and the gas tank is nearing empty—it's not your passenger's job to create gas or to build a gas station for you; nor is it your job to say to yourself, "Why even bother sharing that we are low on gas and I am stressed about finding a gas station? I will just keep it to myself." To the contrary, you should share that you are stressed about not having gas, express how that anxiety makes you feel, and acknowledge to your passenger that you do not expect him to solve your problem (be your savior) but you do want him to know what is going on. In essence, what I am trying to convey is that by withholding what we are experiencing, we block connection, we limit other people's ability to serve as support, and we do not express ourselves authentically. Smothering is one of the forms of being inauthentic; it's looking for a savior. By being vulnerable with your partner and sharing authentically about your anxiety, you take the first step in learning how to save yourself.

Shampoo & Conditioner

On the journey to love, one of the hardest obstacles to overcome is pain. While pain may be a journey that has to be overcome alone, it may also involve another person to bring the pain to completion and restore wholeness. I like to refer to this process as "shampoo and conditioner."

Some days, your hair calls for just shampoo; similarly, pain is sometimes a process that you have to move through alone. To face the source of your pain and move through it to acceptance is enough in itself to restore peace. For instance, if you experienced a traumatic event, you might not need to go back to the person who inflicted the trauma to release the pain—you might instead need to recognize what happened and work through it perhaps through counseling in your faith or traditional forms of therapy; from there, the pain and anguish can be released. Other times, pain calls for shampoo and conditioner; that involves doing self-work through counseling, faith traditions, and changing old patterns of behavior, but it also invites specific person(s)—the co-conspirator(s) of your pain—to be involved in the conversation for full healing to take place and pain to be released.

For example, in my relationship with my father, I came a long way on my own; I went to counseling, read books to help me heal, and found great professional success, but regardless, my pain did not fully heal and peace was not fully restored because my pain was shared by another. As in my relationship with my dad, shampoo and conditioner go hand-in-hand. I had pain from an absent father, and my father had pain from knowing he had not been there for me in the best ways he could.

Over time, I realized that full healing for me could not occur without my dad because the pain was shared. Once I forgave my dad and gave him the opportunity to complete things from the past, that pain was released. In life, we have to acknowledge whether our pain is a "shampoo" or whether it calls for conditioner as well. Pain can be hard to manage; it means facing someone else, meeting shame, guilt, or past neglect in the face, and moving through it. Sometimes, the hardest pain to face can bring the greatest rewards of love and liberation.

You Stepped on My Toe

For years, I thought that once you forgave someone for wrongdoings, that was that, and the whole situation was suddenly resolved. The truth is that forgiveness and pain associated with others' behavior is comparable to when someone steps on your toe.

When a person steps on your toe, typically the individual will be quick to apologize, saying something like, "I'm so sorry; I did not see your foot there." We accept the apology, knowing there was no ill intent in the person's actions and if he would have seen our toe, he would not have stepped on it. We are able to let go of our angst toward that person. While the relationship is healed, what still needs to be attended to is the toe—the toe that now burns and is beginning to ache from being stepped on. While forgiveness has occurred, the pain needs to be managed as well.

For me, this truth hit home in my relationship with my

father. As I mentioned before, offering forgiveness to my father was a large step in my path to healing. But what I did not attend to was the scar tissue that had built up from years and years of perceived neglect and mistreatment.

After years of my father making negative comments about me being overweight and effeminate, and his offering me empty promises, I had the self-worth of a gnat. When people would share how much they thought of me, I heard none of it. I would look to people who were far from emotionally available to attend to my wounds. Their pain met my pain, and nothing but dysfunction followed that equation. The more I found rejection from others, the more and more I gave validity to the years I experienced my father poorly. It was only after I got ahold of the pain and began to attend to the axis of the hurt that I could fully, and authentically, engage in relationships with others.

As with having our toes stepped on, sometimes the first step is to acknowledge the intent behind the impact so we can forgive. Then we can go about the deeper work of attending to the wounds that come as a byproduct of the action.

The Chorus Line

S
o much of my own healing has come about as the result of my finding that chorus line of people who understand my song of pain. In the United States, we categorize people by so many different variables: hair color, sexual orientation, religion, political affiliation, ability, gender, gender expression, native language, and the list goes on and on. Unfortunately, many of these identities can come with heavy weights of pain.

Being black and gay were two of my identities I certainly did not feel held much comfort. At first, being black was not hard since everyone in my immediate family looked like me. Being gay was where I first experienced discomfort. Going to church, where I saw how people looked with judgment upon those who "appeared" to be gay and I heard less than affirming religious messages, which did little to make me feel pride in that identity.

At that time, my mom also carried her own fear about having a gay son. Once, when I was seven or eight, I asked my mom what gay was. I had heard the word used at school in reference to me and was curious what it meant. Upon seeing my mom's facial expression, I realized it was not an identity I wanted to carry, nor was it one that would bring about any good (which I identified as acceptance) in my life.

Years later, upon coming out, I became more accepting of myself and my identity as gay. During this time, though, I realized that I had neglected my black identity at the expense of exploring my sexual orientation. The world of dating in the U.S. as a black gay man allowed me to see that the two identities were not separated. No matter how articulate my words, how well I dressed, or how well I groomed my hair, I found myself being rejected by men who found my milk chocolate complexion less than desirable.

I don't blame others for the rejection; they were just joining the party of self-rejection I was already hosting for myself. After years and years of self-hate and trying to garner the favor of people who could not or did not deserve to hold space with me, I realized it was time for me to find a community that could.

Ten years after first beginning to explore my gay identity, I found the courage and self-awareness I needed to rekindle the conversation about who I was as a black man. I began to do intentional outreach to find community, and I soon found a balm to my pain in a community of people who could sing a similar song of experiences to my own.

The need to find your own chorus line does not just ring true for those who identify themselves as black or gay. I have straight friends and loved ones who come from broken homes, Latino friends who struggle with their weight, Asian friends who come from backgrounds of substance and physical abuse, and white friends who come from working class backgrounds—each with a similar story of feeling as though he or she were not enough. I find that when I shine a light on my identities that I sometimes keep in the dark, and I build community with others who share in those experiences, I cultivate within myself a shelter for love. I move from seeing love as something I need to being a gift I deserve.

In the Wrong Room

I was talking to a friend who was facing the prognosis
of a potentially life-threatening health issue. I asked
her a simple question that had guided my own decision making and that could truly transform the way we
look at events and individuals. I asked her, plainly, if the
prognosis did not come back as she wished, could she find
any peace in the health-threatening news? I have seen family members be diagnosed with cancer and find peace, and
others diagnosed with diseases that threaten the quality of
life find peace. My question to my friend was not "What is
the answer that will make you happy?" It was, "What is the
answer in which you can find some semblance of peace?"
I have come to learn that if the answer does not give you
peace, then you are not thinking correctly about it.

I first learned this principle while studying *A Course in
Miracles*. The idea is that whatever gives you peace is
the answer. The answer that provides peace is not always

"good" news, but rather, it is the news that you can see comes with a purpose. It's the peace that you see so often when people are coming to the end of life—the outcome is not one that can necessarily be perceived as "good," but they enter into a state of acceptance for what lies ahead. If acceptance does not easily come from the answer you are given, then realize you have viewed it incorrectly and need to go back to the drawing board.

Time and again, I have seen this theory prove to be true under the most remarkable circumstances. Once I had two friends who were vying for the same job. One friend called me, delighted that she had received an offer from the company. The second friend, whom I will call Mary, called me later that same day, stressed and filled with anxiety because she had not heard back from the company. I asked Mary what gave her peace. She responded by saying that peace would be brought to her if she would receive the offer on Monday morning. I said, "Then that is your answer." Now, I already knew that my other friend had been offered the job, but I also knew that what brings peace is the answer. On Monday, without fail, Mary called me to say she had been offered the position. Turns out my first friend felt it was not the right opportunity for her, so she turned it down first thing Monday morning, and just like that, my other friend was offered the position. Amazing how life moves.

So when you find yourself filled with anxiety, fear, and deep bouts of sadness, think to yourself, "I have entered the wrong spiritual room." In the wrong room, you seek the wrong spiritual counsel and you make decisions that lead to results that inhibit joy and exacerbate pain. The other room is the room of peace, where the decision feels right, and while you may not have evidence to justify how you feel, it is in that space of clarity that you belong. Your ability to reside in that room of peace without evidence to prove your beliefs is called faith.

Chapter 11

Resilience: Learning to Thrive Despite Pain

Gratitude Despite Pain

One of the hardest things we can do is forgive. Often the road to forgiveness calls for us to overcome the obstacle of hate. I have found the best way to overcome hate is with gratitude.

One time, I was profoundly saddened by a loved one's actions. I felt betrayed and hurt after realizing I had been lied to. I was so overcome by pain that I tried to find any healthy outlet possible to overcome the negative feelings I was harboring. After six months, I began my own process of finding gratitude despite the circumstances. In that six-month period, I forged new friendships, increased my commitment to healthy living, went on several trips to visit friends, strengthened my faith by finding a spiritual community, increased my investment in new activities, and dived deeper into writing the book you are now reading. Yes, a lot occurred in those six months, and until I wrote it all down, I did not realize just how much I had accomplished and how much a series of unfortunate events had led to such moments of fortune.

In that moment of sincere gratitude for the experience, I found the energy and ability to climb over that last cliff of hate to descend safely back to love.

I Don't Look Like What
I've Been Through

All of us have tales of betrayal, hurt, neglect, or abuse. We have all experienced life's forces that did not work in ways we would like. Perhaps it was a job loss, a relationship ending, or a continual financial struggle that disappointed us. Whatever the case, when we learn that we do have complete power and control over how we present ourselves, despite the circumstances, we can put ourselves in a position to see the greatest of manifestations in our life.

I remember being so inspired after watching Beyoncé perform at the Super Bowl. She stood with such confidence and danced with such power that it was awe-inspiring to see. Soon after the Super Bowl, I watched an HBO documentary on Beyoncé's life. It showed the story of her determination and her experiences with loss. The film showed footage of her talking through the experience of a miscarriage and singing from the soul of pain. After the documentary, I reflected on some of the things she shared and other challenges I had learned that she had faced throughout the years. What I gathered from this megastar is that her life has not been a fairy tale. Like all of us, she has experienced her share of loss and disappointment, but when she got on that stage, performed her songs, and danced her routines at the Super Bowl, she looked like a woman full of power, a woman who has seen no harm come her way—a woman who does not look like what she has been through.

As a champion for love, when you own your power, ability, and responsibility to lay no blame on another person or circumstance in determining your actions, then you put yourself in the room of greatest possibility to experience life's greatest abundance.

An Apology Is Not Necessary

Eckhart Tolle, in his book *A New Earth*, speaks to the power of the ego. The ego, the force that moves us in the opposite direction of truth, conjures feelings of fear, pain, and guilt—and tempts us to act in ineffective ways. Often when relationships have hit an impasse, we want to identify our faults in the situation. Sometimes, this can be a healthy practice, serving as an invitation for growth. In other cases, however, this constant searching for answers to our ineffectiveness can actually do more harm than good.

Many times, I have apologized for an impasse in a relationship; I take ownership to a fault and make it all about me (a common practice of the ego). When I do this, I relieve people of the responsibility to take ownership for their part in the relationship. I inhibit growth and make it permissible for others to deflect their own ineffective behavior toward me.

An apology is not always necessary; to the contrary, it may be detrimental to the change we seek in our relationships. This is not to say we don't need to take responsibility for our actions, but sometimes, we have to become aware of when we need to let people sit in their own messes. We are asked to leave others alone to discover for themselves their areas of growth and why certain things happen in their lives. As hard as this practice may be, we must learn to give grace to ourselves and then offer it to others; this can start with the acknowledgment that an apology is not always necessary.

Prosperity in the Midst of Pain

What has brought me peace in life's greatest storms is to find the promise of prosperity in the throes of pain. In each life segment that has introduced me to pain, I have found prosperity in the midst of the trial. When I was getting my Master's degree, I felt the pain of facing past experiences of sexual abuse. Through that pain, I found the courage to come out as gay. When I went into my first professional role, with much success in my position, I found myself in pain and challenged in some of my interpersonal relationships with colleagues. Through that pain, I found the confidence from within to apply to get my Ph.D.

During my Ph.D. experience, when met with many disappointments in relationships and my own journey to cultivate love, the pain of those setbacks provided me with the awareness I needed to forgive my father and restore that relationship. After finishing my Ph.D., when I found myself grappling with life's great questions, when every-thing did not work out the way I planned in my head, and bewilderment was all around me, I found the resolve to begin writing this book. Through each season of pain, I have found the power to manifest prosperity. My story is not shared to boast; it is offered as a testimony that through each of life's tests can come the opportunity to harness our own greatness.

If this book finds you in your own metaphorical storms, I offer for consideration this question: To what end can prosperity be seen in your portrait of pain?

Buyer's Remorse

Recently, I was at dinner celebrating a friend's birthday. One of the other guests shared about her process for buying clothes in department stores. She said she would look at the item and then walk away. If after she left the store, the item was still in her mind, weighing on her heart, then she knew she needed to go back in the store and purchase it. Conversely, she said if she could leave the store without purchasing the item, and ten minutes passed and she was not even thinking about it anymore, then she knew the item was not for her—it was her way of preventing buyer's remorse.

As my friend shared her shopping practices, I began to laugh. The laughter was in my personal understanding that the process she used to describe purchasing things is the same process I believe is used to ascertain our destiny. With love, with people, with career choices, it has always been those things that would not leave my mind that

I knew were part of my destiny. I have met people who, in the course of a couple of minutes, I have known would be integral parts of my life. I would leave them and still have them on my mind. Days, months, years could pass, but I knew our paths would cross again, and sure as day, they always did. Similarly, the thought of writing a book entered my mind years before I opened up the document to start the process.

One time, I had a vision of living in Chicago; months would pass and I would visit other cities, but I always knew one day I would live in Chicago—it never left my thought. Like my friend's process for buying clothes, those thoughts that linger with us are not there by happenstance. Rather, they are put there as whispers to help guide us on our path to our destiny.

Chapter 12

Patience: Combating Fear and Insecurity

.

The Detox

"Patience is a virtue" is an old cliché. However, I have come to see patience less as a virtue and more as a commitment. Like forgiveness and love, patience is a commitment, not a feeling. We can struggle with patience, but it is through our actions that we demonstrate how we are prevailing in that effort.

Once, a friend called me who was in the midst of a hard breakup, with a clear understanding that space was what was needed. She knew that space sometimes is the greatest offering of love we can give someone else, and she was practicing that truth. But in the practice of giving space, she was finding herself riddled with anxiety. On this day when she called me, she was filled with frustration, anxiety, and fear, and she wanted desperately for her former lover to open the flood gates of communication and give her an explanation for their relationship's termination. As my friend talked through her aggravation, I realized she was really struggling less with her ex-boyfriend's failure to communicate than with her inability to be patient. I told her that she could find joy in the fear, anxiety, and frustration she was feeling because it meant that her ability to practice patience was growing.

Impatience is like a drug; we become addicted to the instant need of gratification in whatever form we need it, be it in communication, attention, a change in behavior, or circumstances. In our quest to get our addiction met, we go into action in inauthentic ways, and in the process, we cause more harm than good; in essence, we cause truth to be blurred by fear. When we sit in that anxiety and allow it to be, without moving into action, we can find ourselves at great places of discomfort. But during these moments of discomfort, we can take solace in knowing that our negative feelings are part of the detox process from the drugs of impatience and control. What is certain is that love cannot be fully expressed or find its home without patience.

Love Is Expressed Through Trust

How many times have you been frustrated with someone else's inability to express love fully? Perhaps it's in the person's inability or unwillingness to express his or her feelings, give of his or her time in a meaningful way in the relationship, or through a host of other means. More times than not, the breakdown in love's expression comes from a lack of trust.

A friend of mine recently found herself at a crossroads in her relationship. Her partner expressed his discontentment with the relationship and with her "constant criticism." My friend was at a loss, not understanding where this response was coming from; she felt like she was being blindsided since he had never expressed those feelings in the past. The genesis of the problem was trust. The more she criticized him, the more insecure he felt about himself, and the less he felt he could display his authentic self. As time went on and trust further eroded, his communication about his needs also lessened and so did his expressions of love.

In my own life, I have experienced something on the same scale. I was at an impasse with a loved one; I struggled to understand why our communication was so poor and our relationship never seemed to break new ground. I imagined every reason I could for putting the responsibility for our relationship's failure on the other person. I thought, "If only he would do this or do that, then the relationship would be where I would like it to be, and we could have sanity in our situation." What I failed to realize was my own ineffectiveness in cultivating trust. You see, I suffer from the disease many of us face—not being true to our word. I would often commit to things and then not follow through on those commitments. I would make plans to join someone for dinner or to participate in recreational activities. For one reason or another, and often for good purposes, I would ask to reschedule or cancel altogether. Regardless of how good my reason, each time I did not follow through on my word was another time for trust to be lost and for love's expression to be limited. Certainly, my friend had a role in the relationship as well, and many of the reasons I had calculated for his responsibility in the relationship were valid, but beyond that, I had a responsibility to myself to break my pattern of behavior.

When we verbally communicate our love for someone else, we are making a contract with that person and ourselves. However difficult it may be, and it is guaranteed to be difficult at points, we must learn to stand firm in our commitment to love, even when the other person's love for us is not fully expressed. Love's invitation will often request that we do things we do not want to do, that we face fears, and we leave our comfort zone. Over time, if we understand the power of our word, and our role in others' ability to trust us, we will build the pathway for love's highest expression.

Meet Me Halfway

Communication is highlighted in *A Course in Miracles* as one of the keys to successful relationships. I have always prided myself on my ability to communicate effectively with others. I am able to have difficult conversations with relative ease. I love deep, thought-provoking conversations since that is how I feel the greatest connections with others.

At times, my own strong communication has been to a fault. I expect others to communicate like me, to "go there"—to have deep discussions to forge stronger connections. My expectations would turn to resentments when others did not match my communication patterns. I would become frustrated with others whose conversations with me seemed superficial. But all that changed when I realized that others either are simply not ready or unable to go there in conversation. Like me, many of those whom I struggled to communicate with were looking for a strong connection with me in the same way I was. In fact, others were feeling a strong connection just from being in my presence; for them, the conversation was just an added accessory to the connection they felt by virtue of being around me.

Patience is a gift we give ourselves. When it comes to others' ability to communicate, our greatest gift of love can be seen in our acceptance of others' inability or readiness to go there. Let not our ears make us deaf to love that reaches beyond what can be heard. Truth be told, we can take comfort in knowing that while conversations may not be deep, the love and connection between two people certainly can be.

Chapter 13

Stay the Course

Winning Doesn't Happen by Quitting

The majority of the battle in uncovering love is resisting the urge to quit. In many societies, divorce and separation are the norm—often, we are so enticed by instant gratification and immediate results that we fail to realize that some things, including love, move at a different pace.

Love's expression is grounded in the idea of trust, and trust is cultivated through time—it's an arduous process that requires patience. Of all the things spoken to in this book, trust and patience are two of the hardest points to master. When the relationship no longer seems to have sanity as its purpose and all forces around you are saying, "Quit," stay the course. The main caveat to deciding whether to stay or quit can be found in the question, "Is the relationship compromising my emotional, physical, financial, mental, or spiritual well-being?" If the answer is "No," stay the course.

Irritation, while uncomfortable, is not a reason to quit. Frustration, while often valid, is no reason to quit. At the end of the day, we all must accept that we can't win the game if we quit.

Our Integrity Is Not for Sale

Many definitions have been created to describe the concept of integrity. One of the most basic and time-withstanding is to do what you say you will do.

Often, we profess our love for others, make commitments, and share feelings in a space of sincerity, but without full regard to the magnitude of what we are saying. We see this with marriage. Many people say "'til death do us part," but in the U.S., only roughly 50 percent follow through with that commitment, and while recent data shows that number is increasing, the rate of divorce is still alarmingly high.

All of this boils down to integrity—that force to which, despite other circumstances, we commit ourselves. For me, integrity is the ability to be in action despite feelings to the contrary. In love's greater exercise, we are tempted minute-by-minute, hour-by-hour, and day-by-day to quit.

Our partners, friends, and family can test our every virtue, work on every nerve, and challenge all our foundations of faith.

Despite it all, we are still left with our integrity—our word is our bond. If I say, "I love you," I must acknowledge that "I love you" means "I love you when the times are great and you are loving and courageous to express love in full, and I love you when you are not showing up well for me, when fear has entered into your words and actions, making it hard for you to show up well for me." In either case, you are still 100 percent in control of your space and your integrity.

Integrity is at the root of all success, the core of all healthy relationships. Integrity cannot be sold at the slightest temptation that spurs on fear and doubt.

Temptation

For me, happiness is a temporary state, based largely on feelings. But joy is the sustainable force that withstands life's challenging times.

Temptation always arrives at the hour preceding greatness. Whether it's been in my workouts, in earning my Ph.D., or, at times, in relationships, my greatest moments of temptation have come at the eve of my greatest breakthroughs. We all struggle with temptation. Those urges are just life letting us know we are close to completion—the end is nearing, the marathon is almost complete.

I shared earlier about how I felt called to live in Chicago. Throughout my years in the Ph.D. program, I knew once I completed my degree, I would move to that great city in the Midwest. I would share with anyone who would listen that I was going to move to Chicago when I finished my degree. I would share my prophetic statements with such rousing confidence.

Well, one month before graduation, without a job lined up, my old friend, temptation, came knocking. As I shared before, everyone was telling me to move in a different direction, so when a job opportunity presented itself in another city, I applied and interviewed. Here I was almost at the finish line of my graduate education, for years talking about moving to Chicago, and now I was letting fear put me in a space of temptation. Once I realized I was swimming in the pool of temptation, I immediately signed a lease for a place in Chicago; it was my moment to get out of the pool and fully illustrate not only in words, but also in deeds, my commitment to my faith. A month later, I received the perfect job opportunity for me in Chicago—ultimate prevailing of faith over temptation.

Sometimes in life, we are running a marathon to destiny. We are at mile seventeen of the marathon, well beyond halfway, but far enough from the finish line that we feel the temptation to quit. At this moment, we are called to push through six more miles because by the time we get to mile twenty-three, adrenaline will take us the rest of the way. All we need is to stay the course and not give into temptation because soon the conviction of our faith will see us the rest of the way.

The Treadmill

Every morning, I wake up at 4:45 to head to the gym. My workout ritual starts with twenty minutes on the treadmill. I have been working out faithfully for years now, with running being part of my routine. But all these years later, I still get the same feelings when I am on the treadmill. Halfway through my run, I start thinking, "Am I going to be able to finish? Perhaps I should just quit.... Ten minutes is good, right?" After the run is over, I am wiped. I feel the exhaustion today, just as much as I did when I first started running over ten years ago. I used to get frustrated, thinking, "Why am I still feeling the same after my run now, as I did so many years ago?" What I understand now is that I am running at a different level. The course is steeper, and by the time I finish the run, there is more distance cleared than ten years ago.

I tend to look at negative feelings, such as doubt, anxiety, fear and pain, in the same way that I look at the treadmill.

I wonder why I still have these negative emotions after working and working to continue to better myself. But similar to my runs, my level in life is different; now there is more at stake, and the questions I ponder are different. Life for me is very similar to an exercise regime—it gets harder, my technique and form improve, and my muscles (literal and spiritual) become stronger; thus, more distance is cleared. Now when I feel discouraged, I just look at my level, compare it to the level where I started, and take pride and peace in knowing that while the trek is hard, my growth shows me that I have tenacity, making me worthy of the challenge.

The Forest Is Over

I used to watch the reality TV program *Being Bobby Brown*. It featured singer Bobby Brown and his wife, Whitney Houston.

In one of the episodes, the family goes camping in the woods. After spending a day and a half on the trip, a tired and frustrated Houston looks at her husband and simply says, "The forest is over." Something about this line has stuck with me through the years; it's the simple, declarative nature of the phrase that makes it so infectious. The pursuit of love often requires an impassioned declaration that announces our readiness to end what gives us discomfort so we can give and receive love.

Think of this declaration as a camping trip. You leave your home, with all intentions to camp for just one night. You pack bug spray, canned foods, and your tent to prepare for your adventure. The first night at the campsite, you are nervous, there is a rain and windstorm, so you have to loosen slack in your tent to support the heavy downpour. The next morning, after the rain, you experience a surge of mosquitoes; you have to rely heavily on the bug spray to keep the pests at bay. On the afternoon of day two, you realize you will have to stay another night, so you begin to ration your food supply to last you the additional meals. Night two, it rains again; this time the wind and rain puncture a hole in your tent, causing you to be rained on the whole night while you try to sleep. The morning of day three, you wake up, reflect on your two-day adventure, and say to yourself, "I appreciate this experience; I arrived uncomfortable with the idea of camping, but I not only learned how to pitch a tent, but how to give it slack when rain and wind hit hard. I learned how to utilize my bug spray and to ration meals to last me two full days. God, I appreciate all this learning, but I know I have reached my learning saturation point, and I must declare the forest is over and I am ready to move on to the next chapter of my life."

This situation is similar to how love works. God, that force that is greater than ourselves, is putting us in a position to take stock of the lesson to be learned through our own time "camping." Are we using the nights of rain to learn how to put slack in our tent? Do we see the metaphorical mosquitoes as opportunities to utilize bug spray? And do we see our own strength and resilience when the metaphorical holes appear in our tent and rain seeps in? I invite you to look at what lessons in love, forgiveness, and patience you are being asked to learn. How are you engaging in the classroom of love? What I know for sure is when we take heed of lessons being introduced to us, and work earnestly to be studious pupils in love's classroom, we are then able to declare with great certainty that we have learned the lessons; our gratitude is deep, and the forest of lovelessness is over.

Agitation

I have found three reasons for agitation: It is either an indicator that I need to change the situation, the situation is meant to change me, or the situation is preparing me for something greater. Agitation is typically something we want to rid ourselves of—it's uncomfortable and irritating. However, I have learned that before I rid myself of the agitation, I must determine which of the three categories it falls into. Let's look at each category in a bit more detail:

To change the situation: I remember a time when I was working with a group; it was so hard, but I did all I could to make the environment better. Between clashing personalities and insecurities held by all, it was a challenge that left me at a loss how to respond. I consulted with friends, sought wise counsel, and communicated in the best ways possible to see my needs were met. I knew the group I was working with wasn't where I was supposed to be, but fear of what would lie ahead kept me from moving forward. After years of frustration, I finally had reached a point of saturation where I could do no more in that experience, so I had to leave. The whole point of the agitation was for me to find the courage to take the next big step in my life.

To change me: When I was in graduate school, I went on a staff retreat. The retreat started with an ice breaker called Step Over the Line. During this activity, the facilitator would say a statement (e.g., "Step over the line if you have brown hair.") Those who fit the description in the statement would then take a step over the line. Well, after a series of questions that were light in nature, the questions began to become heavier and more personal. The last statement was, "Step over the line if you have ever been sexually abused, or the victim of sexual violence." At this moment, I found myself agitated. The facilitator, seeing my agitation, asked me what was wrong. After initially resisting answering her question, I finally admitted to being a victim of childhood sexual abuse. Up to that time, I had never admitted it to anyone, but in that moment, I shared it with a group whom I had only known for months. That point of agitation led to the hard and painful journey of reconciling many things in my life and to my coming out as gay. The agitation in that case was meant to change me.

To prepare for something greater: In this case, the something greater was a lesson of forgiveness. One of my best friends grew up with an absent father. Her parents had divorced when she was younger. She had lived most of her life with limited communication with her father. Hurt by her father's neglect, she had deep-seated pain that had gone unresolved for years. As an adult, with a need to heal old hurts, she began the difficult process of reconciling her relationship with her father. This journey called for patience, understanding, and at many points, unconditional love. The journey was full of agitation. A couple of years after she reconciled her relationship with her father, and after years of trying to have kids, she finally became pregnant. She and I soon realized that all of her agitation was preparation for her to be a mother who has mastered patience, understanding, and unconditional love.

Agitation moves in three ways: To call us to change the environment, to change ourselves, or to prepare us for something greater. Now, before I move too quickly to rid myself of agitation, I ask, "What is the purpose behind this?" Without fail, I find the answer; now the courage, discipline, and patience to live that answer…well, that is a different conversation, but the answer is found nonetheless.

When I move *with* agitation as opposed to against it, when I see agitation as an instrument to play in my favor, I find peace, hope, and comfort, despite uncomfortable circumstances.

Chapter 14

Love Is a Commitment, Not a Feeling

Complete the Conversation

Once, I was with a family member, who had just had an argument with her husband. Earlier that day, the husband had left the house to go to work and she had left her wallet in the car. It was not until later in the day, after searching the house all morning, that she realized she might have left her wallet in the car. Panicked and full of fear, she called her husband to see whether her wallet was with him. When he did not answer, she called repeatedly and then proceeded to text him. At this point, she was becoming increasingly frustrated, less and less about the wallet and more and more with her husband's inability to answer the phone.

When her husband called her back an hour later, she was irate. Yelling, she shared her frustration with his inability to pick up the phone, proceeding to put blame on him for her lost wallet. After she got off the phone, we had a conversation to process how she had reacted to her husband over the phone. She realized that her frustration was never with her husband; it resulted from the fear and anxiety that she might have lost her wallet.

Once no longer angry, she wanted to go about the day as if nothing had happened; I explained that she was now being given the invitation to complete the conversation. To complete the conversation with her husband was to admit that she had deflected blame and guilt onto him when he was not the cause of her angst, but in her fear and anxiety, she had made him the target of her frustration. Her initial reaction was, "He already knows; what is the use of saying what he already knows?" I shared that often there are things we already know, but that does not defray the power in the acknowledgment; we can accept responsibility with the understanding that no one is perfect and challenges like this are bound to happen. In addition, what she was being invited to do was speak to her pain and not her complaint. To speak to the pain is to share how we feel about a certain situation or circumstance. In this way, people are better able to receive the information we are sharing. In this case, when she asked, "Why don't you ever answer your phone?" her husband heard criticism and began to shut down. Conversely, if she had shared the cause of her fear and anxiety, her husband would have been better equipped to hear what she was trying to convey. In all critical conversations, ask yourself whether you are speaking to the complaint or to the pain.

After giving it some consideration, she agreed she would complete the conversation with her husband, but she feared he would respond by saying something like, "Yep, you sure did overreact and that was not called for." She was nervous that he would not have empathy, and instead come off with an attitude of, "I was right and you were wrong." I told her the best way to respond to a situation like that was simply to say, "Got it." There are few statements as powerful as "Got it." When we say, "Got it," we are not deflecting responsibility, nor are we pursuing an argument; instead, we are letting the other person know he was heard, we accept responsibility fully, and we acknowledge that responsibility with the individual. In our acceptance of responsibility without pretense or extended conversation, we model a behavior we often want to see from others.

To complete the conversation is hard; it invites integrity and diminishes the ego. But when we are able to complete it, we will see greater connection and manifestation in our relationships.

Showing Love When Other Responses Could be Justified

Ego prompts us that when others hurt us or behave badly, the best way to change the situation is to be tough, tell them off, or just let them know how unacceptable their behavior is. We think that with our demands will come a change in behavior. The reality is that when we attack others, all it does is put up an even larger mask to the love that is there. To show love when we may feel justified in showing anger instead can be hard—it takes courage and real strength—and it's the opposite of what we have been taught.

Many cultures teach that to attack is to show strength while doing the opposite is to be a doormat. This philosophy could not be further from the truth. Real strength comes from the ability to see ineffective behavior and still show love. Can poor choices be addressed? Absolutely. When you address concerns, do it with love rather than hate. For example, Hate would say, "You are a piece of crap and I can't believe you did this to me!" Here is the secret: People who behave like crap toward you already feel like they are crap, so you telling them they are crap is just reinforcing what they already believe. To speak the same concerns in love is to say, "Your behavior is crappy, but you are not crap; your potential is great, so I expect better of you." You see, love sees the truth of who someone is—not the ineffectiveness that is currently being presented by someone. In the end, to see the truth of our connections exposed, we need to learn to respond in love when we may feel justified to behave otherwise.

The Certainty of Love

L ove never dies. If this one truth were believed by all, no one would ever need a self-help book, a dating guru, or another episode of reality television with its false depictions of love.

The certainty that love never dies gives us the security that when mistakes happen, God is already in the mindset of auto-correction. Love is always meant to find its home in the embrace of two human beings. Love is destined, and when it does not meet its fulfillment, it is but a testimony of how we as humans allow fear to overpower faith.

I love hearing stories from older adults; often, their years on earth have provided them with wisdom to understand great truths. I have heard hundreds talk about love and experiencing it with someone else. Each time, I hear stories of betrayal, heartache, deceit, grief, and anger; what I never hear, though, is how the love died. I have heard stories of infidelity, abuse, and mistakes made in passion, but I have never heard how love ended. I have seen relationships end, but I have never seen two people, who found love with each other, see that love end; even when they have separated and found others to spend their lives with, that original love still remains. The secret I have found is that love is a calling, placed on the heart involuntarily—it's a compelling truth that goes beyond the individual. To that end, the act of loving is where choice comes into play. Love's expression is a choice based on our own commitments. Love and our ability to support, foster, and defend that commitment is what showcases our integrity. Today, we use the word "love" a little too freely; we cheapen it, not thinking about the powerful and lasting impact it has. The threat of love invites fear—love is a big thing, so it should be met with responsibility, but the ability to love, and the act of loving, should never produce fear because the investment is guaranteed to display positive results.

On a daily basis, each of us is invited to answer the question: Am I going to act from love, or am I going to act from fear? Fear is the foundation of anger, hate, invulnerability, dishonesty, jealousy, abuse, and betrayal. When we foster fear instead of love, we make the act of loving impossible for ourselves, and for those who have decided to commit themselves to us.

Grace

I will be the first to admit that the pages of this book come with lofty invitations—ideas such as: don't command, demand, and attack, and show love even when other responses may seem appropriate. And then there is the biggest invitation of all: to live in your truth. With every great act comes great consequences, so the journey to love's fullest expression can be arduous at times. This book is like a diet or any strict regimen that we undertake and that differs from the routine to which we are accustomed; it is going to come with inevitable faltering and small failures. It is to be expected that not every word you and I say from this point forward will be full of love. Anger will certainly be part of my vernacular for years to come, and even I, the author of this piece, make demands on others in ways that are ineffective.

Through each of the missteps we take, we should all take comfort in knowing that no matter how hard we fall, we can get back up. I have seen people reach the brink of divorce, find the courage to make change happen, and see their relationships bloom into something they did not know possible. I have seen a family riddled by abuse go from a space of using verbal and physical attacks to try to manipulate behavior, to allowing love to transform their actions. I have seen people plagued by infidelity and distrust find the ability to sing love's great anthem of commitment and faith. In each misstep, and there are many, we are all afforded the opportunity to get back up. The ability to get back up is called grace.

For the parent who has not talked to his or her child in years, for the child who has excommunicated a parent, for the individuals who harbor a hate for a former lover, it is not too late to get back up again. The fall was in the hate, but the rise is in the love. For those who say, "I can't, or it's too hard," I offer that it is not impossible; all are able, and while the act is difficult, it is no more difficult than remaining upon the ground where you continue to lie. Note that as you take this journey, you will fall, and fall again; doubt and the urge to quit will meet you, but know that whenever you fall, you can get back up again, and again, and again.

A Healthy Disregard for the Impossible

Chapter 15

The Power Within to Manifest Our Destiny

Covenant

I f I can't keep my word to myself, how will I ever be able to keep my word consistently with you? When I fully grasped the power of my word, I got a glimpse of my power to manifest my destiny. It took some time, but I finally came to understand the power of my word with others. It took many more years, though, to get the understanding of the power of giving my word in relationship to myself.

I am easily tempted to anger and to move in less than loving ways, so I have to take time to center myself consciously in ways that allow me to be an open, loving person for others. One of those ways I center myself is to take two hours, one evening a month, to sit in a quiet space of self-reflection. I will use this time to journal, read, pray, and do a host of different activities to raise the volume of my own inner voice. Without fail, something will always pop up on my calendar, or a laundry list of household chores will present themselves that tempt me to compromise this sacred time. For a number of years, I would just say to myself, "It's okay; I can just take this personal time next week," or "The five minutes I spent this morning meditating will suffice." It was not until repeatedly failing to keep my word with myself, continually compromising my intentions to have time for myself to accommodate others' desires, that I realized the true impact it was having on my own growth.

I realized I could not fully hold space for my word with other people until I realized the power of my word to myself. When I started saying, "No" to others, so I could say, "Yes" instead to myself, it was a bold shift in the movement to celebrate my own worth.

I can't necessarily control my relationships with other people, but I can certainly control my relationship with myself. Now, I look at the commitments I make to myself as a disciplined training ground for understanding my commitments to others. In many religious traditions, people make covenants with God; in many societies, people make covenants with others in the form of marriage, but no matter the custom or tradition, sometimes the covenant we most often take for granted is the one we make with ourselves.

In Fear I Falter

Fear has been one of the greatest temptations of my life. When I have felt fear, and the temptation to move in another direction, I have always faltered. The falter is less about failure and more about losing the sense of who I am. For me, I find giving favor to fear is like surrendering myself.

When I moved to Chicago after finishing graduate school, I never had felt so called to move to a city. Everything in the core of who I am said I was destined to live in Chicago. As school neared its end and I started to apply for jobs, I was seeing little to no chance for me to make it to my dream city. Friends and family alike were telling me I was out of my mind to limit my job search to just one city. Even my therapist said I should look in multiple locations, and I, for one, think when your therapist says to do something, you should do it.

So I started listening to other people's voices instead of my own. I started applying for jobs in different parts of the United States, and soon after broadening my search, I was offered an interview in another city. Excited about the opportunity to have employment, I said, "Yes" to the interview. As soon as I got off the phone, however, I felt agitation, an inner energy of frustration and angst—I could not put my finger on it. What I have now come to understand is that I was, in that moment, surrendering my truth to fear. In that split second of saying, "Yes" to the interview, I was saying, "No" to my core identity and offering the possibility to lose a little bit of my sense of self in the process.

A couple of hours later, I called the company back, thanked the person I had spoken to for the opportunity to apply for the position, and told him that the job was not meant for me, that the position was destined for someone else, and I did not need to stand in the way of someone else's dream. When I ended the phone call, I felt empowered and at peace; as I mentioned before, peace has always been where the answer lies for me.

A few weeks later, I got a phone call about a job opportunity in Chicago, an opportunity that in many ways was similar to the one I had rejected earlier. I applied, interviewed, and accepted the position. The pathway for me to obtain the position in Chicago was miraculous in and of itself. I had envisioned, six months earlier, working for this organization. In addition, on the day of my interview, my luggage was lost, so all I had to wear to my interview were gym shorts and a polo shirt. After the interview, I called my mom to tell her how the interview went; she thought I was crazy to go to an interview in what was, to say the least, less than professional attire. I replied, "What is destined for me is mine, and it does not matter what I wear or any other superficial things that one can think of; all I need to do is to show up and allow God (the universe, or any other name you use for the force greater than yourself) to open the door." Several days later, I was offered the job.

My own personal compass of truth has never steered me wrong; it is only when I have allowed fear to compromise faith that I have faltered. With love, as with all things in life, we have to ask ourselves to which one we will give our favor—it's either faith or fear, but it can't be both. All those around you may have a sense of what is right for you, but we all must love ourselves enough to trust in our own inner voice, to silence all the noise, and to bring defeat to the tempter known as fear.

Destiny Deferred

As I mentioned before, in every experience, I ask myself the question, "What is the lesson this moment has to offer?" I love that question because when it is asked with sincerity, then at some point in the future, the question will be answered. Each time the question is answered, it is life acknowledging that we are one step closer to our destiny. I must be honest; most times when I ask the question, it is often at the darkest hour, when pain is evident, despair has taken company with me, and hope seems to be nowhere in sight.

My thought in those hard times often is to quit or move in a different direction. Sometimes in the heat of anger or disappointment, I don't want to ask the question. I just want the situation to end quickly. When I fall into the temptation to omit the opportunity to reflect on the lesson and just to move quickly in a new direction to squelch the difficult feelings, so often I have come back to realizing I am deferring my destiny.

Think of this matter as like being a kid who is dreaming of becoming a doctor. Your whole life, you imagined yourself practicing medicine. Then you reach your second year of medical school, with classes and course work consuming your time, so you become frustrated with the process. Seeing friends who are out having a good time and enjoying life, you become bitter and decide to quit to gain your time back and regain a perceived life that you feel is being compromised by school. In the moment you quit, you are deferring your destiny. Rather than leave school, ask yourself, "What is the lesson in this moment?" It could be that rather than be a specialized surgeon, you want to be a general physician who has more manageable hours and less of a school commitment than a physician in a specialized area. You may learn, through the sacrifice of time, how precious each moment is, and when you do have free time again, how you will maximize it with those you love most. Whatever the answer may be, you won't know until you ask the question, "What is the lesson this moment has to offer?"

A great act in the process of loving ourselves is to develop an understanding of how our actions either substantiate, or compromise, the materialization of our destiny.

Chapter 16

Allowing Our Intentions to Meet Our Purpose

Timuel Black

I once attended a program that featured Civil Rights leader, Timuel Black. Beyond the powerful stories Black offered, one thing in particular he said has stuck with me for years. Black said, "In life, we must notice when we can't hear what people are saying because what they are doing is speaking so loud." I love that quote, perhaps because it hits home in regards to my own hypocritical nature at times.

I have been known to profess love to a person one minute and yell at him or her the next. I would share my desire to pursue a relationship with a particular person one minute, and as soon as that was not reciprocated, I would be on to looking for someone new. *A Course in Miracles* posits as its primary function to see us bring about the release of fear. The book goes on to share that all prayers are answered, so when we feel as though a request has been made but not been heard, we need to look at where fear is present. I'll admit that when I first read this principle, I thought, "What the hell does that mean?" After several reads, what I understood was that prayers may seem unanswered because fear is prevailing in our lives.

I would pray for dynamic changes in relationships, but when people did not behave the way I wanted them to, I would either get angry or leave—the classic fight or flight. Here I was, praying for transformation, but doing all I could in my actions to counteract that prayer…all of it based in fear—my fear being that people would not change their behavior, so I would try to manipulate them to change, or lacking faith, I would just quit altogether.

What is a hard truth now for me to swallow is that Black was 100 percent right. When our actions are speaking so loudly (most often out of fear), sometimes it is hard for God to hear our request. What is asked of us for our prayers to be answered is the courage to move despite fear, to take a stand for our beliefs, and to be consistent in our practice of expressing love. If we can do that, we will demonstrate the powerful effectiveness of prayer because when we make large requests, we will see incredible results in return.

When Deeds Speak,
Words Are Nothing

S o many books, songs, and poems have been written about the concept of love. We speak of love as a feeling, the sputtering in the "heart," the space where we are lost for words in the arms of a lover. The truth is, love is the furthest thing from a feeling; love is a commitment. Love is that space where our words meet deeds in consistent practice. It is one thing to speak of love; it is another entirely to see it in action.

Recently, a friend and I decided to embark on a book discussion group. The original plan was that we would meet every Sunday for thirteen weeks, discussing one chapter a week. Week one was great, but then week two, it was, "Can we move the book club discussion to another day?" Week three was, "I can't do this week; can we do two chapters next week?" Then week six, it was, "I have a migraine; can we do next week? " Then week eight, "I can't do this week; can we do two chapters next week?" By this point, my love tank was on empty. I felt my time was not valued, nor did I feel the space we were looking to create was meeting the expectations we had discussed.

I fall guilty of this same crime all the time—I say one thing and do another. I constantly find myself in a space where I am inconsistent in my words and deeds. We often wonder why our relationships fail, or why we don't see the forward progression we so often hope for.... The answer is simple and lies in the way we express our words, in the way we take those words and put them into action. As the old African proverb says, "When deeds speak, words are nothing."

Courage Is Contagious

When I am out for a run, I have the terrible habit of illegally crossing at intersections. I can clearly see that the caution sign is saying, "Stop," but in the midst of a good run, with a great song blaring, I just let adrenaline kick in and lose all foresight of what the consequences could be. Each time I cross, without fail, two or three others will follow suit; it has become amusing to watch. What the followers of my bad behavior show me is that courage begets courage. Now, I am not arguing that all courage is intelligent; I am simply postulating that courage is movement despite fear. Certainly, I know (and have a bit of fear) that I can be hit by a car, but I cross the street anyway.

The crosswalk is also a metaphor for how when we are courageous, we invite others to be the same. I have often had to ask myself what courage calls me to do in this moment. Sometimes, courage is asking me to be in action, while at other moments, it is asking me to be still. The latter, being still, is a lesson I am just starting to master. Growing up, I was so used to being in action to manifest results. If I wanted to go to college, I had to be in action and make good grades; if I wanted to lose weight, I had to be in action and go to the gym. Alas, love does not follow the same laws as preparing for college or changing fitness strategies. Love, at the most dynamic levels, is calling us to move in discomfort, to listen to courage's calling and see where it leads us.

If you are like me, and you are quick to agitate a situation to bring about change, where taking control in your life is something you have just been conditioned to do, perhaps love is calling you to be still. The Beatles were on to something when they said, "Let It Be."

On the other hand, if you move in a more passive manner, often looking to others to provide you the answer, perhaps love's invitation is calling you to be in action and display levels of control you may not have thought possible. What I know for sure is that when I move in fear and take action, when love is calling me to stand still, I bring about a paralysis in those I love most; I limit their ability to profess love to me.

Self-Sabotaging Behavior

At the same time I was writing this book, I was working with a web designer on a website that would complement the conversations in this work. Being busy with multiple projects, my web designer would often have to come late for meetings or reschedule. On one occasion, we had set a date to meet, then rescheduled, and then rescheduled a second time. When he approached me about rescheduling for the third time, he asked whether we could meet on the weekend because it would provide him greater flexibility and more time for him to show me the extensive work he had done. In an angry and frustrated place, I responded that I was not able to meet on Saturday. In my head, I had perfect rationale; it was summer in Chicago, and I wanted to hit the beach. Truth be told, the weather report had called for rain, and I was being contrary, trying to get back at him for not remaining committed to our original two dates. In my head (listening to my ego), I thought, "I will show him; if he can't make my timeline, I certainly will not make his."

Here I was, committed to having a website complete; I had been working on this project for months and was so excited to see the fruits of that labor. But now, rather than meeting my heart's desire, I was more interested in proving a point. Soon after emailing him back about my inability to meet, I realized I was engaging in self-sabotaging behavior—I was acting in a way that directly counteracted what I wanted. Fortunately, I caught myself in that moment. I called the web designer back and shared that I could in fact meet that day—we wound up having an incredibly productive conversation.

I realized that the way I was disengaging from my web designer was the same way I would disengage from others. For example, if I called my best friend and he did not call me back, then I would call again. And if he still didn't return my phone call, then two weeks later, when I ultimately got a return call and he left a voicemail apologizing for the delay, my initial thought would be, "I am not going to call him back—I will show him! How dare he disregard my messages like that, and go two weeks without calling me back." I would go into telling myself a tailspin story of how I was a victim. In honesty, I called him the first time because I wanted to talk to him; I called the second time because I wanted to talk to him, and now that he was available to speak, I did not want to be in conversation—the epitome of self-sabotaging behavior. There is no greater barrier to the truth than anger. Every time our actions are counter to what we express as our deepest heart's desires, we are just giving clear indication to God that we do not yet have the capacity to hold those gifts that are part of our prayer's request.

Conversely, when we move beyond ego and feelings of anger to react in direct alignment with our heart's desire, we open space to see the truth in situations, restore peace within ourselves, and move forward in the manifestation of our destiny.

Being a Safe Harbor

On the path to actualizing love, we can become impatient, asking why certain events are happening, or why certain things are not working. What we eventually learn is that life is just preparing us to be a safe harbor for the ships that bring us what we want.

I remember at one of my lowest points on love's great journey, I was distraught and frustrated, wondering why things were not moving as I had intended. Then the answer came to me: power. In that moment, I began to acknowledge that I had given my power over to someone I loved. When he called, I was happy; when we did not speak, I was devastated; at every crossing, I would question whether or not love really existed between us. In my fear and doubt, I realized it was not the love I was questioning; it was the power I had arbitrarily given him.

I then started the process to reclaim my power. It was a slow, tedious process of putting myself in uncomfortable situations, reclaiming my life for myself, and seeing the joy that existed beyond my relationship with a particular person. Consider creating a weeklong plan of action to reclaim your power. For some, reclaiming your power might look like working out, going out for drinks with friends, confronting pain, or going to places (physically and emotionally) that challenge your comfort zone. Whatever it may be, when you begin the process of going there, you will see liberation on the other side. When the problem looks too large to resolve and the situation seems to challenge all sense of hope and faith, ask the simple question: What am I to do today? Then slowly you will see the change of your heart's desire.

The Harvest

When I was younger, I remember elders in my family often saying, "You reap what you sow." For the longest time, I thought this phrase was just about sowing seeds of wrongdoing and the wrath that came from them. All these years later, I realize to reap what you sow is not based in harm or good; it's based in fact. When we sow love, peace, and compassion—love, peace, and compassion is what we find in return. When we sow hate, revenge, and scornful behavior, that, too, we will reap.

Joel Osteen once spoke of God's grace being like a bamboo plant; it takes years for the roots of a bamboo plant to settle; it will look like no growth is occurring, but in year five, the plant can shoot to above eighty feet. I love this parable because the same is true for the seeds we sow in our own lives. So often I have been tempted to move in a direction outside of love. I have been given seeds by others' ineffective deeds—the seeds of vengefulness, attack, and ill will. We all have, at one time or another, been given these seeds, and it's up to us whether we decide to sow them. I know for myself, despite the temptation, I meditate and work earnestly only to plant seeds of love.

We all can admit to falling short on this kind of planting from time to time, but what I know for sure is that despite circumstances that may arise, all of our seeds (good or bad) will come to bear fruit, and it will be incumbent upon us to accept the harvest of the seeds we have sown.

Your Crown Is Not Crooked

We all have a destiny, a calling that is placed on our lives of what it is we are supposed to be. For some, it comes from spending hours in the kitchen doting over food that is prepared with love. For others, it is getting on a stage and dancing in front of others, where they are left moved by the experience of seeing that expression. Whatever destiny is calling you, it is your throne from which to rule over all the goodness life has to offer you.

While writing this book, I experienced some of the greatest personal difficulties and disappointments I have ever known. Many days, it took all the energy I could muster to perform my daily functions—I felt as though I were Bill Murray reliving Groundhog Day; every day was the same, without passion and without full expression of joy. While I was in a season of pain, mainly inspired by my disappointment in others, I knew I could not let others' actions define my power. I had to learn to move beyond others' intimidation or inability to show love in ways that worked best for me. I knew the calling placed in my spirit, the destiny I was meant to fulfill, and from that throne, I could not allow my emotions to overpower my ability to succeed.

What I hope to offer the reader for consideration is: Your crown is not crooked. Your throne of destiny is not defined by relationship failures, others' inability to be there for you, or others' unwillingness to offer you love. Your throne and your crown are both maintained and straightened by the power you harness within to move beyond blame so you can situate yourself in your own truth. It is when we live in that truth, and take actions accordingly, that we see our resentment diminish when others do not meet our expectations.

Chapter 17

The Promise of Faith, The Power of Possibility

Grab Hold of Faith

Without faith, extraordinary things are not possible. In a biblical context, faith is described as, "the substance of things hoped for, evidence of things not yet seen." Regardless of your religious (or non-religious) tradition, each of us is asked, or rather invited, to a place of faith if we are truly looking to see love manifest in our lives.

A Course in Miracles describes that often where we experience the most fear is where love is also most present. In simple terms, the ones we love the most, are those same people who offer us the experience of the greatest fear. The only weapon to combat fear is faith. It is in that space of faith that we can show patience when intolerance seems permissible, where we show love in the face of the temptation to quit, where we offer compassion when the voice to attack is looming. It is in faith that we find solace when love's presence seems hard to find. It is in faith that we get up and prepare our spiritual home for intimate love, when there seems to be no resident in sight.

Above all things, we are asked to have faith; for it is in our faith that we testify to our love for others. All of us can find a mate: someone who is "safe" that does exactly what we ask, who follows every rule book play we have created in the sport of love, and who will give us every predictable outcome we desire. But to find a mate who stirs your soul, transforms you and your lived experience, well, that will only be done by faith. Doubt, fear, and anxiety are the tools used by the ego to distract from the possibility and promise around the corner—so whenever the trifecta of doubt, fear, and anxiety come your way, grab hold of faith, knowing that the promised land of peace, joy, abundance, and love are eagerly awaiting your arrival after this chapter of learning and self-discovery is complete.

The Miracle Assessment

I have a test that has proven to work in my life, and I invite you to consider it in your own life. Whenever I find myself in a relationship where I am frustrated because things are not moving the way I would like, I do the miracle test. I take the relationship in context of where it was to where it currently stands. If, when I do that, I can say the difference is a miracle—that something positive occurred in the relationship that I never would have expected—then I know I am on the right path. Whenever you can say that, stay the course.

For example, say you are trying to lose weight. After shedding many pounds, when you look back on where you were to where you are now, if you can say, "Wow! That's a miracle," then stay the course. When you have children and they are frustrating you, but you look back on their prior actions compared to their actions now, if you can say, "Wow! That's a miracle," then stay the course. Staying the course after recognition of a miracle is the acknowledgment that breakthroughs are possible and always occurring, even when we don't see them.

Patience is a virtue, so when I find that I either want to demand, command, or attack someone to get him to change his behavior, or I want to abandon the relationship, I set a date six months to a year out from that pinnacle point of frustration. For that period, I commit to showing love; I commit to liberating others, by not commanding, demanding, or attacking. If at the end of this time, the relationship has not moved, or if it seems as though movement is not likely to happen, I then decide whether to set a new marker or move in a different direction. Without fail, every time I have made this practice a habit and I have acknowledged miraculous moments along the way, I see those moments continue to happen.

Waiting for a breakthrough in a relationship is hard; at times, it can be like watching a plant grow—you can't see the growth, but the roots are taking form, and sooner rather than later, height and blooms will showcase the transformation that originally was sealed in your faith.

The Small Things

W e dream and envision grand ideas of what our life should and can be. As we move along our journey, we can become distracted and frustrated when we don't see our visions manifest. What I have come to understand is that life's miraculous moments are in the small things; they happen all the time, and those small things are what lead to the big movements of our dreams.

At times, I would become so frustrated with my relationships and why they were not moving in the direction I envisioned. When I would sit in this space of anger and frustration, I would often forget the small things—the "wins" that were happening along the way. These small wins are life affirmations that we are moving in the right direction, to stay the course and recommit. Now, whenever I experience the small things, I immediately journal—to take stock of the moment, the small truth that was realized that will lead to the breakthrough I desire.

This book is one of those great breakthroughs. It was one fall Sunday afternoon when I first sat down to begin the process of writing this book. Not being a writer by trade, to say the process was intimidating is an understatement. But slowly, I saw small wins, first, at a dinner party with friends, where I was introduced to resources that supported writers who were considering authoring a book. Then, there was the call with a friend about potentially developing a website. At the same time, I had committed to writing for fifteen minutes each day. What started out as two pages, over time turned into over a hundred; what started as a concept of a website turned into a webpage, and what started out as a lofty dream (a two-page document) of writing a book is what you see before you now.

Another story of small wins is the biblical story of Noah and his small wins that led to miraculous moments. Noah had a grand vision of an ark that would sail the earth for forty days as the world was struck by heavy rain—a grand vision in anyone's estimate. Noah received the vision seventy-five years before the rain came. Imagine having a grand vision that takes seventy-five years to manifest! How did Noah stay the course? He celebrated the small wins. You see, Noah was able to recognize how the vegetation had changed, giving him the necessary materials to build his ark; he noticed how the birds shifted migration patterns to support his vision of all species of animals being on the ark. It was through Noah's recognition of small wins that he was able to persevere and solidify his truth.

For many of us, love is like the great story of Noah. Love often does not reveal itself all at once. For many, love is coaxed in fear and mistrust from past hurts. For those of us brave enough to follow love's vision, we must be vigilant to love's whisper—when small wins are made, we must note them and refer back to them often to support us in staying the course until that promised day when love's great flood arrives.

Not Yet

I was once about to fly to a friend's wedding in Boston. Running late, I got to the airport about fifteen minutes before my plane was scheduled to take off. I hurried through security and rushed to the gate, only to get there five minutes after the plane took off. I was so frazzled and stressed that I would not make it in time for the wedding. Fortunately, I was rebooked on another flight, but when I arrived at the hotel, I realized my iPad was missing. It occurred to me that somewhere during the day in all the hastiness, I had taken my iPad out of my bag and forgotten to put it back. Frantic, I called the airline, both airports, and the police department. I filed a claim, and then I said one of my favorite prayers. I said, "God of many names, you always answer prayers in one of three ways, 'Yes,' 'Not yet,' and 'I have something better in mind.' I have lost my iPad and I need to ensure its safe return."

The next day, I followed up with the airline, the airports,

and the police department...yet still no iPad had been turned in. The last day of my trip, we were set to go sightseeing. I, still being stressed from losing my iPad, was in no place to see the sights and sounds of the city. I shared with my friends that in my anxiety-ridden state, I would be no fun to be around. I suggested that if we could go by the airport before sightseeing, perhaps I could find some comfort in making one last ditch effort to retrieve my iPad. My friends conceded.

We went to the airport, and I first went to the airline and inquired about my iPad; they said it was not there and suggested I go to the airport lost and found. There, too, I received the same response. The lost and found offered one final solution—that I go to the airport police station.

At this point, I decided to go back to God. I said, "God of many names, you always answer prayers in one of three ways: 'Yes,' 'Not yet,' and 'I have something better in mind.' I appreciate the answer 'Not yet' since it gave me an opportunity to see how I can be careless with my things, allowing emotions of anxiety and franticness to get in the way of me being present." I went on to tell God how I knew no new iPad was in my future, so something better in mind was not an option. I concluded my conversation with God, declaring that my iPad would be at the police station.

When I arrived at the airport police station, I asked the clerk at the counter whether an iPad was there. She said, "No." I said, "Ma'am, I need you at least to check your store closet and see if anything is there because I know God answers prayers in one of three ways, and I believe my iPad is here." A couple of minutes later, she came back with a surprised look on her face and said, "If there were an iPad here, how would I know it was yours?" I said, "Turn it on, click on the mail icon, and you will see my name appear." Five minutes later, she returned with my iPad.

It's that type of radical belief that all things work in our favor that sustains me through life's great difficulties. Like my iPad, the inquiry into love presents us with the opportunity to hear "No" often, but like my lost iPad, the answer is never really "No." It is always "I have something better in mind," or "Not yet."

So, whenever we are faced with a "No," that is not the moment to quit in discouragement, to surrender in despair, or to throw up the flag of defeat. Rather each "No" should be seen as preparation for our closing arguments to God about what we are learning in this season of "Not yet."

The Picnic

The week leading up to my sister's wedding was full of angst and anxiety. My sister, feeling all the energy and magnitude of the moment ahead of her, had all sorts of questions and doubts. I told my sister that her marriage was a manifestation of her destiny. You see, my sister and future brother-in-law had seen much struggle and hardship on their own journey of love. I had seen firsthand how they had helped one another grow, and that each one had been shaped for the better by knowing the other.

To me, it was clear my sister was fulfilling her destiny and purpose by getting married. When my sister called me with all of her doubts and fears, I shared with her that our destiny is like a picnic scheduled for one o'clock in the afternoon. I told her the rain always happens before the picnic. I told her that it was ten o'clock in the morning (metaphorically speaking), rain clouds had set in, and the showers of the morning were causing her doubt and anxiety. I reminded her that it was not one o'clock yet, and she couldn't allow the weather of ten o'clock to distract her from the picnic that was destined for the afternoon.

A week later, the day of my sister's wedding was full of overcast skies, metaphorically and literally. Her wedding was set to take place at five o'clock in the afternoon, but around three o'clock, the overcast skies turned into heavy rain showers. My sister became distraught, trying to figure out how she could hold her planned outdoor wedding in the rain. I said to her, "Sister, it's three o'clock; your wedding is at five o'clock, and just like the picnic I spoke about the week before, the rain always comes right before the picnic." As sure as life's guarantee, at 4:30, the rain clouds lifted, the sky cleared, and my sister had the most gorgeous outdoor wedding.

At seven o'clock that evening at her reception, I went up to my sister and asked her how the picnic was. She laughed, reflecting on all the angst, pain, fear, and anxiety she had felt the week and hours leading up to her wedding. All of that negative energy had been for nothing, and the wedding that she had questioned so much had turned out to be the most beautiful of occasions.

When we listen for our truth, what we are seeking is an understanding of our destiny and purpose. Once we have that understanding, it is like the picnic set at one o'clock; it is promised to occur. Like my sister's wedding and the metaphorical picnic, it is bound to rain, introducing us to doubt and questioning everything we hold to be true. At that moment, when we are about to give into despair, like at three o'clock the day of my sister's wedding, let us remember that it is not five o'clock yet, and rain always comes before the picnic. Stay the course and keep the faith.

When the Answer Is "Yes"

I shared before the popular phrase that God answers prayers in three ways: "Yes," "Not yet," and "I have something better in mind." Most of what is written in this book is about the "Not yet," but I would be remiss if I did not think about that invitation to consider when the answer is transformed into a "Yes."

I believe love is like a teenager praying for a new car. The kid prays and prays, dreams of what the car will look like, even sharing with friends how much this car will bring joy to his life. Friends of this kid say things like, "Wow! That would be awesome," or "I hope you get it!"—words of encouragement that instill a sense of faith while the young teen waits to see whether the car will come to fruition. What is rarely asked is, "What happens after you get the car?" We don't ask about how the person's driving skills are, or where she will park the car, or what she will do when she goes off to college—will the school even allow her to have a car her first year of college? These are all great questions that reside in the land of "Yes."

We see movies and television shows with their fantasized portrayals of love. Those who are single and looking for love watch these movies and television shows with a sense of longing. What we rarely ask is: What happens on the day your prayer for love turns into a "Yes"? Are you ready for the responsibility of committing to love with another person? Are you ready for a life that is full of compromise and including another person in discussions on life's big topics? These are big questions, worthy of the life we all are capable of leading. So while we sit dreaming of the love of the future, worrying over "Will it arrive?" consider changing that narrative, spending less time pondering the "if," and more time preparing for the "when."

The Fourth Grade

I had the most amazing fourth grade teacher. Mrs. Whitt was her name, and she was the greatest teacher I could have asked for; it turns out she was also one of my greatest mentors in understanding love. As a young child, I had very little value for education; I would do just enough to get by, and receiving mediocre to downright poor grades did not matter much to me. I remember when I got my report card with all As, Bs, and one F, I was so delighted, excited by what I thought was a stellar report card. "Only one F," I thought—it seemed to be an all around success to me. That day, Mrs. Whitt sat me down and asked me what I thought of my grades; she did not share my delight in them. She said she knew I could do better, and there wasn't any pride I should take in failing one of my subjects. Mrs. Whitt, in her serious, stern, yet loving tone, showed me a potential I did not see in myself.

Throughout the rest of that academic year, Mrs. Whitt would

continue to challenge me; she showed me love despite my mishaps and how my grades would fluctuate from good to awful. Through it all, Mrs. Whitt never questioned my potential, remaining firm in standing for the kind of student she knew I could be, and talked to me as the bright child she saw me as and not the mediocre student I presented myself to be. Those early childhood lessons would be some of my biggest indicators of how to love others.

A Course in Miracles speaks to the special people put in our lives to help us through our journey. Each of us will be introduced to someone who will need an accurate mirror of who he or she is in the same way Mrs. Whitt was that mirror for me. Several times throughout this book, I have talked about the principle of refraining from commanding, demanding, and attacking; before, I mentioned that principle as a way to continue sustained growth in relationships, but it also serves the purpose of fostering the salvation of someone else.

Salvation is that transformative way of being that allows people to be authentic and fully expressed versions of themselves. Salvation is what Mrs. Whitt offered to me when she saw my potential and found loving ways to support me in finding that same potential for myself. I continued to struggle throughout that school year, but when I went on to the fifth grade, I earned nothing lower than a B, and then I went on to finish high school, graduate from college, complete a master's degree, and attain a Ph.D.—this all from a kid who did not learn to speak until nearly age five, struggled throughout early elementary school, and almost failed the third grade. Mrs. Whitt was more than a teacher of math, reading, and science; she was a teacher who spoke to others' potential, an instructor of love, and a magnificent instructor at that. Life will give us all our own metaphorical classroom to teach love when we are offered that student (or students). That student could be in the form of a friend, a partner, spouse, or child; whoever he or she is, I pray you are inspired by what Mrs. Whitt did for me to lend your faith to see the possibility in and empower someone else.

The Invitation

I n my life, I have seen nothing that has transformed my relationships and the ability to express love more fully than the invitation. The invitation is the moment when I have found enough self-worth to muster the courage to say what it is I need to say, not from a place of anger, but from a place of love. When I offer the invitation to others, I am acknowledging my commitment to them by sharing openly, and my commitment to myself by recognizing that my voice is one that is worthy to be heard.

When I was growing up, my dad would often criticize me; he would talk about my weight, effeminate disposition, and my posture. I took his feedback like it was gold, the truth, the gospel. My father's criticisms continued well into my adult years, until one day I had had enough. I decided I was going to share with my dad, face-to-face, the impact his continuous criticism had on me. I met with my dad, shared that I knew deep inside that he wanted us to have a good relationship, and acknowledged many other challenges that had marked our relationship in the past. I told him that his intentions were not met with possibility when he continued to criticize me. I shared that I can only think people are rude who criticize me constantly, and I knew he did not want me to think of him in that way.

The words I shared were not from ill intent; they were not words of comfort either. They were simply expressions of the truth. Up to that point, I had complained to everyone else about my father, but I had never harnessed the courage to have the conversation with him. That day was the beginning of transformation; it was the opportunity I seized to let go of resentment because I had finally expressed myself. That day was a training ground because my dad will not be the last person I will have to invite to have a courageous conversation.

Since that day, my dad has never said a critical word to me. In addition, I have realized that my dad saw his critical feedback as coaching. He saw his criticism as a challenge presented to me to rise to my greatest potential; he saw it as a way to build connection. I was left asking myself, "Why did it take me so long to have the conversation with my father?" Part of the answer is that I played my father small. I would talk myself out of it, saying he would get mad, or he would not be able to hear what I had to say, all of which possibly could have been true, but I would never know unless I provided him the opportunity to show me himself. Looking back, the conversation could have ended in no other way but positive. Even if my dad had responded negatively or refused to meet with me, it would have just been an acknowledgment that his intention to have a loving relationship with me was contradictory to his actions, and I had provided him the invitation to move forward with his intentions, but he had declined, so I could let it go.

This situation is no different than a friend who often speaks about losing weight, but when you invite him to the gym, he declines. When intentions are not met with actions, you have done your part to support the person's desires, so now you can let it go. When we give people the invitation to hear our authentic voice being shared, when we speak our truth, we give light to the opportunity to transform our relationships and ourselves.

The Color Purple

I want to close with one of my favorite tales of love: the story of Celie and Mister from Alice Walker's book, *The Color Purple*.

For those who do not know the story, Celie grew up with a hard life; she finds herself married off to a man (an arranged marriage, in a lesser sense) whose first wife died, and he is looking for someone to take care of his kids. Their marriage is volatile; Celie's husband, who is referred to as Mister for the better part of the book, abuses her physically, verbally, and emotionally. When I first saw the film adaptation of the book, I thought, "Wow! Mister is a terrible person." I questioned how he could be so abusive to a woman who was so caring. I thought he resented her for being something she was not; what I later came to understand was that he loved her deeply. I understood the immensity of his love for her when I thought about central figures in my own life. At times, I would get so angry that I would want to yell and scream at those who behaved poorly toward me. Many times, I felt as if I were being treated like shit (for lack of better words). Then I realized that people cannot cook up experiences of shit for me to taste unless they have been to the culinary school of shit themselves. In that fact, I found grace.

The Color Purple illustrates this truth so well; at one point, Celie finally finds the courage to leave her husband. As she is getting in the car, about to make her escape, he yells at her, taunting her and degrading her as a person. At first glance, you see Mister's rant with Celie as the work of an evil man, but beyond that, at the deeper spiritual level, is a man who is making a desperate (and albeit ineffective) attempt to beg a woman whom he loves to stay.

She simply replies, "Everything you done to me, already been done to you." That ideology of: "I was shit on, so I shit on others" is the essence of the pathology of pain. It is what Celie experienced with her husband; it's what millions of people experience in bad relationships; it's what millions of children experience with ineffective caregivers. We don't have to know other people's journeys to understand their pain; we just need to see how they love others and how they love themselves…that will share more than their words ever will.

The essence of this book is not to question where love is present. Rather, what the reader is asked to figure out is a person's ability to express that love. It's not accurate to question whether Mister loved Celie, for that, at several points, is evident. What is left to question is his ability to express that love effectively.

As Celie was leaving, she could have called Mister all kinds of names and attacked and demanded things from him, but she didn't—never once in that moment did she call him anything but his name, which showed she was practicing forgiveness.

Every story in this book has been considered through the lens of forgiveness. Forgiveness is the ultimate spiritual exercise a person can undertake—it's in that place where all truth resides and we are offered the necessary guidance to respond properly to other people's pain.

I share my deepest gratitude to you for joining me on what I pray has been a journey for you of enlightenment on your own path. Recently, I read Kamal Ravikant's book *Love Yourself*. Ravikant ends the book by acknowledging that his book may not hold your truth, but whatever your passage to truth is, you must commit to it and not waver. Like Ravikant, I acknowledge that this book is not the universal truth, but I pray that those who read it at the very least find some morsel of knowledge for their own journeys. Whatever the case, never lose your zest to search all things to find truth because what I know for sure is that love is a gift we all seek; we do all we can to find it, and when we do find its invitation, I pray our hearts, minds, and spirits are prepared to receive it.

Afterword

Thank you once again for joining me in this conversation. If you have found this text helpful, don't let it end here; share it. Let others know what you enjoyed about this book. Tell coworkers, friends, family, significant others, and anyone else about the stories that resonated with you. Visit www. TheInvitationToLove.com to share your own stories of love.

In addition, you can share directly with me how this book has supported your journey. On the pages that follow, you will find direct ways to connect with me and join the conversation about The Invitation to Love.

This book was conceived in love, prayed over with love, and delivered to you with all that love in total. May that same love be with you from this point forward.

God Bless,

Darren Pierre, Ph.D.

Continue the Conversation

There is no better way to bring the stories in *The Invitation to Love* to life than to have Darren himself come share with you his understanding of love and its triumph over difficult circumstances.

Darren has spoken to audiences of various sizes and has been noted for his inspirational, engaging, and unique approach that uses stories and metaphors to simplify complex topics. He is able to deliver a broad message across diverse populations, suited to meet the audience's needs. Darren has been described by others as inspiring, a teacher at heart, and someone who brings his whole self to his work and invites others to do the same.

In each conversation, Darren intends to leave people moved, equipped, and inspired to make manifest their deepest desires.

To learn more about opportunities
to have Darren speak,
email booking@theinvitationtolove.com,
or visit the website
www.TheInvitationToLove.com